SCARECROW
in a Melon Patch

Scarecrow
in a Melon Patch

A Memoir

Judge John Ward

Copyright 2023 by John Ward.
All rights reserved. All rights reserved. No part of this book may be reproduced in any form, except for brief passages quoted within reviews, without the express written consent of the author:

>John Ward
>homeward02@yahoo.com

ISBN: 979-8-9879632-0-3

Cover illustration: Wendy Ward Mara
Book and cover design: H. K. Stewart

Printed in the United States of America

This book is printed on archival-quality paper that meets requirements of the American National Standard for Information Sciences, Permanence of Paper, Printed Library Materials, ANSI Z39.48-1984.

Dedicated to the men and women of
the **Gideons International**, who seek no recognition
in this world but desire only the approval of the
risen Christ and the joy of seeing lost people find
new lives in Him. They are humble, special people.
I love them dearly.

Contents

Acknowledgments 11

Prologue 15

1. My Dad 17

2. Uncle Charley 18

3. The Hangin' Judge 22

4. Charley Myers 24

5. The Shoe Factory 27

6. Warren, Arkansas 30

7. Fayetteville 36

8. Little Rock 38

9. Sam Laser 39

10. Morrilton 42

11. The Idol Broken 47

12. God's Hand 50

13. Life Changes 52

14. The Beginning 54

15. Legal Research 57
16. Renewal 60
17. CBMC 62
18. Dave Parr 65
19. The Gideons 67
20. Teresa 71
21. Africa 73
22. The Legislature 83
23. Judge Digby 90
24. On the Bench 91
25. International Challenge 94
26. God's Promise 97
27. Asia 99
28. Beautiful Feet 107
29. Davao 113
30. Getting Healed 116
31. Death Row 118
32. Jack 122
33. Malasia 124
34. Borneo 127
35. South America 132

36. Bolivia 133

37. Peru 140

38. Brazil 147

39. Dr. James Thomas 150

40. International Chaplain 153

41. Sioux City or Sioux Falls? 155

42. Telling Others 158

43. The Command 160

44. The Candidates 162

45. The Conversation 164

46. Conversation Barriers 167

47. The Building Contractor 170

48. The IRS Agent.....................................174

49. God Has a Sense of Humor 177

Epilogue 181

About the Author 183

Acknowledgments

This book was possible with the kind help of Gary Green, my lawyer friend who introduced me to the talented book producer, H.K. Stewart, who edited along with my wife, Kerry Ward, and my son, Jeffrey Ward. My artist daughter, Wendy Ward Mara, who produced the cover art, and my other daughter, Kerry Ward Baxter, who guided our tech needs along the way, were also essential. Thank you to those and others who encouraged me to write it. I offer gratitude to my God, who lifted me from the quagmire of my own early life decisions.

*For the customs of the peoples are worthless;
they cut a tree out of the forest, and a craftsman
shapes it with his chisel. They adorn it with silver
and gold; they fasten it with hammer and nails so
it will not totter. Like a scarecrow in a melon patch,
their idols cannot speak; they must be carried
because they cannot walk. Do not fear them; they can
do no harm; nor can they do any good.*

Jeremiah 10:3–5

Prologue

For the first 30 years of my life, I worked hard to construct my idol. Poured years of labor, time, and money into building it. I relied on it to lift me out of mediocrity and onto that tier of those I respected and envied. I had no idea at the time that what I was constructing could not, in fact, help me at all. It was not until the little Black lady with the tattered purse came to my law office for an interview that I discovered it. She had the courage say to me, "You're not very happy, are you?" then handed me a little green New Testament. I never thought that would lead me to a complete reversal of my goals, but it did. I would later come to realize my effort to become a big, rich, hotshot lawyer was exactly like the Scarecrow in the Melon Patch that Jeremiah described so perfectly. Hammered and nailed so it would not totter. It was worthless to ever be something worth worshipping, much less to live or die for, which I came to realize is the measure of a true goal.

The Scarecrow lured me away from my family, my friends, and the richness of knowing Jesus as my best friend, who has led me on an unbelievable excursion. It was Jesus who dared me to try things much bigger than I could have dreamed on my own. It was He who taught me that people who live within their own capabilities miss the reason why the Holy Spirit was given to us. We could have done ordinary things on our own without Him.

My ardent hope and reason for writing this is that one man or woman will give up the Scarecrow idol and go all in with the God who formed us and gave us supernatural power to do incredible things. Those which we can look back on and ask ourselves how we could have been a part of them. Lives that were changed, including our own.

1. My Dad

"Church is for women and sissies." That's what my father told me from time to time as I was growing up in Fort Smith, Arkansas. He slept late on Sundays, so I went with my mother and sisters to First Baptist Church. They went for worship, I went because my buddies were there and we were inseparable. After we got home, my father had me load the military jeep he had bought after the war, and we headed for Greenwood, a little town 15 miles away where the beautiful hills and streams abounded with fish and wildlife.

He had served on the *USS Savo Island* aircraft carrier in nine major battles of World War II in the South Pacific, and had lost 50 pounds in the two years away. Before he left, he was a jolly man, six feet four and well over 200 pounds. When he came home, he was sullen, bad tempered, sick with diabetes and what we now know as PTSD. He seemed to find no peace outside the hills of Arkansas, and we could find no peace with him at home for the nine years he stayed with us after returning from his service. He eventually left my mother, sisters, and me, and I was not to hear from him for 20 years.

2. Uncle Charley

My grandfather Charley Myers had been a well-known lawman in Fort Smith in the years following the career of Judge Isaac Parker, the United States district judge who had brought law and order to Fort Smith and the Indian Territory. By the time I knew him well, my grandfather was pot-bellied and limped badly, but always basked in his incredible reputation as the man who had captured some bad men.

Now, he was but the county jailer affectionately known as "Uncle Charley" to everyone in Sebastian County. As a young man he and his brother Bill had been coal miners in Hartford, Arkansas, where they had met Ben Sewell, part Cherokee, who became their best friend. When they moved to Fort Smith, the brothers opened Bill and Charley's Bar on Texas Corner, and Ben Sewell was the quiet peacekeeper in the bar. He was a tall man with huge hands and well capable of handling whatever situation arose in the rowdy bar.

My grandfather had told me when the three of them were working the mines in Hartford, there had been a terrible explosion that killed several men. Ben Sewell had risked his life by crawling deep into the mine and dragging a man to safety only to kill him weeks later during a card game, suspecting him of cheating. He hadn't been prosecuted. I suppose the community felt the man's life belonged to Ben who had once philosophized, "One of the greatest tragedies in life is there are folks with closets full of clothes and not a drop of whiskey in the house." Bill, Charley, and Ben were tough men you didn't want to mess with, hardworking and hard drinking.

Charley Myers, foreground, in his drinking days.

Ben had a beautiful family member, Cora, who worked in the mine store in Hartford, and my grandfather Charley fell in love with her. But she was a Godly woman and wanted no part of Charley Myers. Later, she agreed to marry him if he quit drinking, which he promised to do.

They married and Charley lasted two months before coming home drunk and rowdy. Cora's Cherokee blood boiled and she hit him in the head with a plate, opening a huge gash over his eye. An amazing event given that Cora was maybe 105 pounds and Charley was a big man. But she put the fear of God in him, and that was the last drink of any liquor he ever took. They closed Bill and Charley's Bar, and he started attending church, becoming a staunch Christian, always sitting four rows back on the right-hand side in the First Baptist Church. Now a deputy sheriff, people couldn't believe the change in him.

The different Charley Myers holding daughter Kathleen (my mother) with son Roy, wife Cora, and Goldeen (my aunt)

With his newfound faith he became a strong supporter of law and order, for which there was much need in Fort Smith. From its beginning it had been a wild and lawless area, but the crime was mostly what would be expected in a frontier town of bars, prostitution, and the smaller crimes that go with them. But the end of the Civil War had brought a period of more intense lawlessness with more infamous crimes—murders, robberies, and rapes—exploding in the area. Outlaws found their escape easy by crossing the Arkansas River into the Indian Territory where no law could be found and lawmen were hesitant to pursue them.

3. The Hangin' Judge

Isaac Charles Parker was born in Ohio on October 15, 1838, and at age 17 began an apprenticeship reading law with a well-known law firm. Passing the Ohio bar exam at age 21, he joined his uncle's well-established law firm in St. Joseph, Missouri. Loving law, politics, and public service, he was elected city attorney, serving until the Civil War broke out. Believing slavery was simply wrong, he chose the Union side. After the war, he renewed his love of law and politics and started his own law firm. He was both a gifted lawyer and a spellbinding speaker, which advanced him quickly from county prosecutor to judge of the Twelfth Missouri Circuit Court. Continuing his rise, he was elected to the United States House of Representatives where he stood firmly for those causes that were lacking of support in Congress at the time. He pressed for pensions for veterans, women's rights, and the organization of Indian Territories with their own governments. He was passionate about helping people who had no representation and needed help. His push for the underserved made him unpopular with some, so he chose not to run for re-election, asking President Lincoln for an appointment to a United States district court.

For someone who was known as the "Hangin' Judge," Isaac Parker was in fact a compassionate man. Lucky for Fort Smith, Arkansas, Parker turned down the offer to serve in Utah and accepted the office of United States District Judge for the Western District of Arkansas, which included the Indian Territory. He commissioned Bass Reeves as Deputy United States Marshall, who became one of the first African American U.S. marshalls.

With the coming of Judge Parker, empowered by the United States government and a desire to clean up the rampant crime, things improved. With the help of Bass Reeves and other deputy marshalls, who dared to retrieve the worst criminals from the Indian Territory, the area became a safer place for its citizens. For all his reputation as a judge who hanged, he actually favored the abolition of the death penalty. He tried 13,490 cases in his time on the bench, of which only 79 defendants were hanged. Given that he was trying some of the most notorious criminals in the territory, he probably should have been known as the "judge with heart."

4. Charley Myers

Charley Myers, born in 1865, came to Fort Smith in 1905, just nine years after Judge Parker's 21-year term ended. Through his years in law enforcement, and as lowly night jailer, the change in his life had been dramatic, from rough and tough bar owner to a man who cared about everyone he met. Years later I realized how much the change in his life had made such a difference in mine, and how he changed so dramatically. Charley Myers had been a deputy sheriff for Sebastian County and later a detective with the World Association of Detectives that took up some of the slack for Judge Parker, bravely retrieving many notorious criminals out of the Indian Territory, now Oklahoma.

When I wasn't in school, I hung out at the jail with my grandfather, listening to stories told by him and the inmates who mostly were the town winos. They would spend 30 days in jail, go out and get drunk, and hope to get arrested early in the evening before Uncle Charley served the dinner meal. I can still smell the bologna cups filled with mashed potatoes and that distinct smell that permeated everything in the jail.

Every Tuesday, the lawyers would show up and talk to their "clients." They were ordered by the local judge to represent the indigent, who were mostly just a bunch of guys who couldn't cope with life and chose to live out their days on steel cots behind bars. The cell doors were always open, and it was a strange but happy family. They could count on an extra slice of bread from Uncle Charley.

Charley Myers, third from right, returns from a successful hunt for Oklahoma fugitives with World Association Detectives.

In the summers, I would sit on the bunks by my inmate buddies, waiting for Charley to get off work. The lawyers would show up in their silk suits and two-toned shoes and tell their clients what they were facing the next day in court. Everyone knew the judge would waive the fines and clear the jail. No doubt the lawyers' fine suits and shoes made an indelible impression on me, and I decided I wanted to be a big, rich, hotshot lawyer when I grew up. I liked their confidence. They had life by the tail.

Nobody in my family had ever gone to college, and I knew if I were to get an education, it would be on my own. So, I got a job at the White Spot, the legendary local hamburger joint, where I showed up at six every morning to face 40 pounds of onions that needed to be peeled and grated. The White Spot had figured out that grated onions piled on the grilling burgers created an aroma that was irresistible for miles. I always cried during the grating process, having tried all the local remedies for preventing tears to no avail. When the last onion was done it was time to go to school.

When I got to school, I could sit anywhere I wanted, clearing whole rows. I saved every penny, and my grandmother promised she would send me $5.00 a week if I went to a Baptist college. It was my only option. Before leaving, my grandfather told me he had met God, who has a plan for all of us. I remember filing that away, aware that something amazing had turned him from being a drunk to a respected law man. I attributed it to Cora's opening his head with a plate.

5. The Shoe Factory

At Ouachita Baptist University, named for the tribe that roamed the Caddo valley on the Caddo River in Arkadelphia, Arkansas, I discovered I hadn't saved enough to pay for the first full year. Building on my other part-time work experience selling ads at the *Fort Smith Times Record* newspaper, I went to the owner of the *Siftings Herald* to seek work. In those days, ads were made up using "mats" that depicted women in dresses, men in suits, and other items usually found in newspaper ads. The raised parts of the mats transferred ink to the press and left the intended image on newspapers.

To the left of the front entrance was a pile of mats that obviously hadn't been sorted in years. I was told I could work on commission based on the increase in weekly ads that were submitted by the small businesses, which hadn't changed in years. Pouring through the mats, I developed larger and more attractive ads that local merchants were happy to see, but reluctant to buy until they were told of the larger ones being planned by their competitors. The advertising doubled and commissions sufficient to pay for college that year came in. But the owner decided I wasn't needed since the ads were now regularly selling. I was a victim of my own success.

Ouachita Baptist College, now a university, has for several years been named by *U.S. News and World Report* as the best small college in its multi-state district. When I attended, its speech and drama departments were headed by Dr. Dennis Holt, internationally acclaimed as an insightful adapter of Shakespeare and a passionate director. After the Siftings no longer needed an advertising manager, I was hired by the school to assist Dr. Holt to design and build sets for his plays, receiving a school credit of 50 cents an hour with no limitation on the number of hours. I shifted majors to speech, learning pubic speaking from Dennis Holt, and to political science, a department headed by Dr. Bob Riley, who had been blinded at the battle of Bougainville and moved around the campus with a white cane.

Riley's vocabulary was broad and compelling and his knowledge of history and politics nothing short of amazing. His wife Claudia, read regularly to him, and their reading list included the 140 massive volumes of the *Arkansas Reports* containing cases reported from the Supreme Court of Arkansas. He made the law come alive and confirmed my goal to be a hotshot lawyer.

In class, he would often recite the names of cases from old volumes that related to the political situation we were covering. I was fascinated by him and still treasure the times in his living room, together with Claudia and the students who shared a love of learning at the master's feet. He was later elected lieutenant governor of the state and served as governor in the governor's absence. In one absence, "Governor Riley" appointed me a special justice to the Supreme Court of Arkansas.

Ouachita College was known as the "shoe factory," since many students fell in love and graduated as pairs. My "other shoe," Berdell Cahoon, the "Tiger Day Queen," was a sophomore when I was a senior. She was a devout Christian, and I called myself one, due to meeting my buddies each Sunday at church. We were cast in *Death of a Salesman*, I as Biff Loman, and she, cast against type, as one of the shady girls. During the run of the play, we fell deeply in love. Ignoring her parents' advice to wait until her graduation, we married after I graduated and we moved to Warren, Arkansas, where I had gotten a teaching job. She could drive our new Volkswagen back and forth to Ouachita to finish her last year. Our plan was for me to enter law school after our year in Warren. She graduated *Magna Cum Laude* in three years, even with the increased class loads needed to graduate early. We were laughing one day about college grades. She said, "I only made one B in my whole college career." I remember saying, "Big deal. So did I." But her other grades had been on the higher side of the B.

6. Warren, Arkansas

We rented one of two upstairs apartments in a beautiful antebellum home across from the high school in Warren, owned by a widow with strict rules. She explained she had rented the other apartment to a couple of Mormon boys and there was no separate entrance into their side. They must go through our dining room to get to theirs and we should be circumspect at all times. We became fast friends with the two fine young men, but years later were sure that on each occasion when they came through, we had added to their worldly education.

Warren was a small town situated in southeast Arkansas amid miles of beautiful dense forests, most of which were owned by Potlatch Industries for their lumber business. Of equal importance was the production of the famous Warren Pink Tomatoes. A few families were the staunch backbones of the community, which was close-knit, but hospitable and helpful to any in need.

In Warren, I went to the superintendent's office to sign a contract for the upcoming year. The school accommodated grades eight through 12 and my contract provided for five classes covering each of the grades. The contract included the option, for a slight extra pay, to drive a school bus each morning and after school. Since Berdell was to leave early each morning for her commute to school and arrive back later in the afternoon, I agreed to drive the bus. Due to my lack of seniority, I was assigned to Route Five with the oldest and slowest bus on the lot. Route five was 26 miles round trip on dirt roads taking students to and from school. The bus seated 40 and had a top speed of 22 miles an hour. I don't want to brag here, but with the bus assignment and teaching, I was to earn $360 a month.

The bus experience was fun and educational. On the dirt roads outside of Warren, folks made a living off of the land, including year-round deer hunting, fishing, and farming. Sometimes they had disagreements and some families feuded. It wasn't uncommon to see a man plowing with a sidearm tucked in his belt. But mostly it was harmless stuff and I grew to love the kids, except on my early-morning route when they got on the bus with sidemeat and other non-tantalizing sack lunches before I had enjoyed breakfast.

After signing the contract, I learned that the teacher whose place I was taking had been tossed out of his class window on the first floor at the end of the school year by some over-happy boys. Though uninjured he opted not to return. I was advised by the superintendent that I should make a call to Fred Murphy, a fellow teacher, who got along well with the students and who might give me some pointers on surviving the year. I would be inheriting some of the boys who had pitched the teacher.

Crossing the street to our furnished apartment I found our phone on a table, but was confounded by the lack of a dial on it. I picked up the receiver and heard the operator say, "What number, please?"

I had been given Fred's number, which was only four digits, and said, "Two, two, seven, one."

Immediately the operator said, "Fred's fishing."

I said, "I beg your pardon?"

She said, "You're the new teacher, aren't you? Are you trying to reach Fred Murphy?" I conceded I was, and she said, "He's fishing this afternoon, but he'll be home probably around five."

Little did I know this would be the beginning of one of the best years of my life. That very year was the unveiling of *The Andy Griffith Show*, and I was in Mayberry.

Fred met with me and gave some curious advice, something he had wanted to try himself with a difficult class. "On the first day of school, go into the classroom before the students arrive, place a metal wastebasket in the front of the room and be five minutes late to class. When you arrive, they'll be loud and having fun. Walk up to the wastebasket and give it a kick. It'll make a huge noise, and the room will be immediately quiet. Wait a few seconds, and say, 'I know you tossed your teacher out of the window last year, so I'm going to give you five minutes to throw me out, if you can.'" I took the advice. I was sweating bullets, but issued the challenge. The guys must have thought I had a black belt or was a professional boxer and I had no takers. We went on to have a great year. The seniors turned out to be wonderfully enjoyable students and I was elected Senior Class Co-Sponsor.

With that honor I volunteered to direct the junior and senior class plays, coach the tennis team, and sing a solo at a performance of *The Messiah* at Christmas. While loving Warren, my goal of being a lawyer never left my mind. At the end of the school year, Berdell needed to attend summer school to graduate, and I needed to make enough in the summer to pay for a move to law school, which seemed to be a dim prospect in this small town.

Warren had a movie theater, a Dairy Queen, and a pool hall, but little else for entertainment, especially for families. I had enjoyed going to a miniature golf course in Fort Smith and had the idea that one would succeed in Warren. I would need to find a lot, design a course, build and light it. Nothing seemed impossible and everything fell into place. My father-in-law, Bert, lived an hour away and was an electrician with building skills. We only needed a flat lot to rent.

In the middle of town was a large enough lot with houses on either side. I discovered it was owned by an elderly widow who lived in a local hotel in summers. She was a gracious and friendly woman who agreed that the young people in town needed a miniature golf course for entertainment. We made an oral agreement for $25 a month rent. The Par-Tee-Putt golf course was taking shape. Zoning was never mentioned by anyone.

Parallel one-by-six pine boards were built as side rails. Sawdust, when spread on bare ground then smoothed, makes a great putting surface, and a local hardwood business had mounds of left-over sawdust. Bert and I erected four-by-four light poles and lighted the course. Hazards were built using whatever things we happened to find, but all worked amazingly well.

The course opened and the people of the town flocked to play. There must have been a huge need for a place for young families to congregate and visit as it became a community success. On the Fourth of July we made $125, a small fortune. But one afternoon I arrived to find a deputy erecting "No Parking" signs for blocks around the course. The deputy, who seemed sympathetic, said some of the merchants in town were upset. They were losing business and wanted the signs posted. The deputy suggested I go by the widow's hotel and tell her what was happening.

Looking forlorn, I explained our plight to my landlady. She listened thoughtfully, and said, "You go back to the golf course, and we'll see if I can help."

When I arrived back at the course later, the signs were being taken down. The deputy explained that the widow owned many of the buildings in town and had obviously made some calls to the right people. We had a great summer, and I was able to sell the golf course for $2,000, enough to finance our move to law school and put money in the bank.

In the middle of summer, I drove to Baton Rouge, Louisiana, to take the LSAT for entrance into law school. Louisiana State University was the closest place to take the exam before school started in the fall, and I needed to make a high score on the test to get into law school at the University of Kansas School of Law in Lawrence. We started there because my brother-in-law was the superintendent of schools in Bonner Springs, Kansas, and was able to assist Berdell in getting a teaching job. Everything fell into place as we had come to expect that it would.

After the first year of law school my studies had to be placed on hold as we were expecting a child and I needed to work. I got a job at Mobil Oil Company in Kansas City in the credit card center, and we had a delightful year with the arrival of our son, Jeff. I was offered a promotion at Mobil, but law school was still in our plans. We were homesick for our home state, and I was accepted into the University of Arkansas School of Law at Fayetteville.

7. Fayetteville

Berdell signed a contract to teach in West Fork, a rural school five miles out of Fayetteville, and I found work at Red Ball Moving Company making a dollar an hour. I often worked 40 hours a week while going to school, and it was a hard year. My partner who drove the moving van was small but strong. When he opened his lunch pail each noon, it contained only a half-pint of whiskey. He drank it all each noon. I was amazed that he could expend so much energy moving heavy things. I offered him some water from my thermos to help wash it down, but he declined the offer. "Don't want to build a fire just to put it out," he said. Berdell began to pray that I could find a less demanding job so I would have time to study and go to church with her on Sundays. Her prayer, not mine.

At the beginning of my senior year, I was given the incredible opportunity to be a part-time research assistant for the newly formed Arkansas Judiciary Commission, created by the legislature to study the Arkansas judicial system and make recommendations for a better working system. The position paid $10 an hour, and I was to attend monthly commission meetings in Little Rock and take research assignments from the commissioners. The new job and big raise were a blessing since our daughter Wendy came along at that time.

One of the commissioners was a fine lawyer from Fayetteville, and we formed a good working relationship. Following graduation from law school, and while studying for the bar examination, I received a call from Justice Sam Robinson of the Supreme Court of Arkansas. He had been searching for a law clerk, and my lawyer friend in Fayetteville had recommended he call me. What a stroke of good luck, I thought, as top law firms often sought associates from the ranks of Supreme Court clerks. Berdell had been praying for a job for me, and I had to agree our lives did seem to be moving under a plan. But I was reluctant to credit anything to God. More to my hard work.

8. Little Rock

Justice Sam Robinson had been a smart, hard-nosed prosecutor in Lake Village, Arkansas, before his election to the Supreme Court, and he gave me broad latitude in assisting with cases assigned to him. I soon found great interest in civil law and enjoyed seeing the lawyers perform in oral arguments before the court. Trial work was fascinating to me because a lawyer had to make quick decisions on his feet and be able to communicate well with jurors. While my exposure to trial work came only from reading transcripts of trials, I quickly decided being a trial lawyer was my calling. Before the year ended, I received a call from one of the outstanding trial lawyers in Little Rock, offering a job as an associate in the firm, which did trial work for most of the largest insurance companies. I accepted before asking what it paid.

9. Sam Laser

At this point I decided I'd be the first one in the law office each morning and the last one to leave. That would impress them. This, of course, required that I ask Berdell to take on the task of raising my son and new daughter while I went about the business of becoming a big, rich, hotshot lawyer. She was smart and would do a great job, and I wanted to be a partner in the firm as soon as possible. The challenge was that one of the guys came in at seven each morning and another didn't leave until seven in the evening. But I had set my course and didn't deviate from it.

Trial work was just as fulfilling as I had hoped, and with each new case came an increased desire to win. At the feet of Sam Laser, one of the best trial lawyers in the state, I learned the skill of communicating with jurors.

"Never use notes when making your closing arguments. Talk from the heart," my mentor insisted, and "If you lie to jurors, they will know it instantly." I was able to win some cases I probably shouldn't have.

After two years, Sam called me into his office and said "Congratulations, John, we're making you a partner. Why not slow down a bit? You've got a long time to practice law." I was not about to slow down. Besides, our daughter Kerry had joined the family, and with a wife and three children I felt an even greater need to produce.

While we were primarily a defense firm, one of my partners and I took on a wrongful death case representing the estate of a young nurse who was killed when a large truck, being towed by a smaller one, crossed the median and hit her car head-on. Her husband ran a service station in a small town where they lived and she had commuted to work each morning to the capital city. She worked for a plastic surgeon and had been impressed by his skill in restoring normal smiles to cleft-palate children. As a result, she and her husband had taken in a foster child with a cleft palate, and, while the surgeon donated his services, she was working to pay the other costs that attended the surgical repair of her foster daughter. They also had adopted a child.

The company that owned the truck that caused the accident was a large wholesale whiskey distributor that had a gruff owner. Some said he had a bad temper. The case was hotly contested, the owner strongly denying fault. I was given the assignment of cross- examining him after he testified for the defense. "See if he really is hot tempered," my partner challenged. I'd read his deposition so many times I had memorized and footnoted the possible conflicts expected in his direct testimony.

On direct, he stated when he saw the towed truck swaying, he eased the brakes on. But I remembered in his deposition, he said when he saw the truck swaying, he had "put the brakes on real hard." Normally, I would have handled this by bringing the error to his attention and asking if he was mistaken then, or mistaken now. But charged with testing his temper, I asked, "Were you lying then, or are you lying now?" The question angered him, and he jumped from the witness chair, swore at me, and stormed out the door. The judge had the bailiff retrieve him. He did indeed have a hot temper.

A record verdict for the death of a working housewife and mother was the result of a mother's compassion and great character. We had made new law that foster children and adopted children could recover for the death of a foster or adoptive parent. That verdict drew other plaintiff's cases. We were doing well on both sides of the courtroom, plaintiff and defendant.

10. Morrilton

While bragging to a partner who specialized in criminal defense, I opined that anyone who had skill with a civil jury could be equally successful in criminal defenses. On a bet, I took on the next criminal case, which turned out to be a murder in a small town. According to the bet, my partner had to keep me abreast of the applicable criminal law at trial. If we won, he would concede that good lawyers could handle criminal or civil cases. If we lost, I would concede it took special skills for criminal matters and that civil lawyers weren't up to it.

He laid out the case for me. Three young men in our city, who were friends, all in their early 20s and without criminal records, had an acquaintance who claimed to know a man in a small town outside the capital city who grew high quality marijuana on a farm. The three young men pooled their money, $1,000, and asked the acquaintance to see if he could buy some.

As a background, the small-town grower was a man who weighed over 300 pounds, had served time in Angola

Prison, and was a dangerous character. He was photographed in his A-frame house in the country with his new marijuana crop, with two full ammunition bandoliers crossing his bare, hairy chest and two young topless women at his side. He always carried a 30-caliber automatic weapon and had been arrested by the local sheriff several times, but the witnesses always decided not to show up for testimony. The sheriff told me the last time he had the man in jail, he had taken a shard of glass and carved "Baby Raper" in his cellmate's back. He was a rough customer.

When the buyer arrived on his motorcycle with $1,000 for pot, he was met on the porch and brought inside. He offered to buy, but the seller was not of a mind to sell. Instead, he took the money and forced the buyer to lie down on the floor, where as a warning, he outlined him with 30-caliber bullets. "Don't come back," he said.

When told of this story, the three young men made a plan to go to the small town and retrieve their money or the pot. They equipped a van with rifles, handguns, and a bolt cutter. After several months of planning, the day arrived for the journey to the small town 40 miles away.

As they arrived at the property, one young man stepped out 100 yards from the house, rifle in hand, and moved through the woods closer to the A-frame. The other two in the white van stopped in front. The big man stepped out on his front deck, 30-caliber rifle in hand, and asked their business. One of the young men bravely got out and said they had come for their money or their pot. The big guy laughed, and the shooting began. Shots were coming from inside the A-frame and from the big guy's weapon. The young men fired back; the big guy was hit and staggered

70 feet before falling dead. The young men left in a hurry, but the local sheriff met them on a dirt road and arrested them. According to the sheriff, all three confessed in writing to the crime. They were offered a deal, but one didn't like it and hired us to defend him.

Our young man had never been in trouble, not even a speeding ticket. His parents were divorced, but he had other wonderful family support, including his mother and grandmother, who was a pillar in the church. He was a talented marksman and hunter. The bullet that had done the killing had passed through the dealer's heart and lungs. The defendant denied firing the shot.

The trial was set, but we were to learn the problems attendant with defending an out-of-towner accused of killing a local in a small town. While the decedent had a reputation as a very bad man, his parents, who lived in the town, were decent and respected in the community. Nobody in the town wanted to give us any information, which was a problem. Our defense was self-defense, which required us to prove the decedent was the aggressor, or had a reputation as an aggressor. While the sheriff could prove this for us, he warned me not to issue a subpoena for him to testify at the trial or I would regret it. I had no choice and issued the subpoena. The sheriff was now our enemy. Understandable, given the decedent's family were stalwart local citizens.

The trial lasted three weeks. Tensions were high each morning as we drove into town. People were glaring at us. Armed deputies were placed around town as a precaution. Jury selection consisted of questioning in a small room with just a prospective juror, the prosecutor, and our team, including the defendant. We had decided to opt for as many female jurors as possible and to be very careful with the men. Selection progressed, but one man we had selected made me nervous. He claimed to be a bi-vocational pastor in a local church that was affiliated with the same denomination as our defendant's grandmother. It seemed a bit too convenient. We were to regret his selection.

Hundreds of exhibits were introduced by the prosecutor, whose primary witness was the deputy who had showed up at the scene, interviewed witnesses, and taken photos. The deputy testified that there were hundreds of shell casings found at the scene, but none were 30-caliber fitting the decedent's rifle, indicating the decedent hadn't fired and thus was not the aggressor. Then there was the matter of the signed confession, which stated the young men had planned the trip for months and had intended to retrieve their money or the pot, no matter what. The prosecutor opened the case by having several deputies bring in all the guns and the bolt cutter the young men had taken with them, piling them on a table in front of the jury. Things didn't look good.

To his credit, the sheriff testified truthfully, establishing that the decedent could be a violent man. That he had arrested him several times without a conviction, given the fearfulness of witnesses. He reluctantly agreed the decedent had a reputation for being an aggressor.

We called the guru of ballistics recently retired from the State Police. The van used by the boys had a clean bullet hole through the left rearview mirror. Our expert, who had been used many times by the prosecutor, testified that the clean hole was definitely from a 30-caliber. We had removed the mirror from the van and allowed the jury to examine it.

Because of the deputy's testimony, we needed to account for the missing 30-caliber casings. In one of the photos taken by the sheriff, the deck in front of the A-frame, where the dealer had originally stood, had wide gaps in the plank flooring, and it was dark underneath them. By suggesting to the jury that any 30-caliber casings must have fallen through the gaps, we were able to skirt the issue that someone had disposed of any casings. The deputy testified he hadn't looked under the deck.

The prosecutor wouldn't budge from his offer of 40 years if our man pled guilty, but our client refused. The jury had been out for most of four days, and it was looking better for us. I was told the longer a criminal jury is out, the better for the defense. On the fourth day, the negotiations began, with our client refusing 30 years, then 20. Finally, we were able to get the prosecutor to agree to a sentence of one year, and the deal was done. We found out later 11 jurors wanted to acquit our young man, and the only holdout had been one man.

Our client was a model prisoner and was out in eight months. He has owned his own business and been a model citizen for years since. There was a genuine dispute between my partner and me as to whether the case had been won or lost, but I confessed that having the young man's life in my hands had gotten to me, and I never wanted to try another criminal case again.

11. The Idol Broken

I had satisfied my desire to be a good trial lawyer, but the cost had been too great. While my wife had done a great job with the children, I had missed precious time with the family.

After each victory, I stayed out late celebrating with the guys. When late coming home, my dinner was always warming in the oven and I would eat alone and get up early to start again. Often, I wouldn't see my family in the mornings.

While I knew lots of men, I had no close friends, or ones to tell just how lonely and miserable my life had become. That was to change dramatically.

Coming home late one night, I bypassed the dinner in the oven, went through the dark house to the recreation room where I sat on the floor to remove my shoes. As my eyes got used to the darkness, I saw balloons hanging from the ceiling and a large paper sign stretched across the wall that said, "Happy Birthday." They had celebrated a birthday, and I had missed it. I struggled to remember whose birthday it had been when it occurred to me that it had not only been my wife's birthday, but also my youngest daughter's, who shared her birth date. My dream as a big-shot lawyer had become a nightmare. How could I have traded a relationship with my family for such a cheap goal?

I went out on the front porch and sat on the steps. It was 2:30 a.m. Looking into the sky, as men often do in despair, I wanted to negotiate a settlement of the mess I had made. But the other side was silent. Looking across the street I noticed the home of a very successful building contractor, who was a kind man and who always seemed to be at peace with the world. Knowing Ernie's light would come on at 5:30, as it always did, I waited.

When the light came on, I knocked on his door, and Ernie quickly answered. "John, hey, what's going on? How are you?" I must have looked bad. Up all night, no shave, smelling bad, but Ernie was cordial as always and invited me in. "Mable," he said, "John's here, come on in." Mable was a sweet woman, often showing kindness to the neighbors, and she joined us on the couch. "What is it, John?" Ernie said.

"I need to talk," I said. "I've just missed my wife and daughter's birthdays. I've made a big mess of things. I thought you could help. I'm not happy."

Ernie was quiet for a moment, then said kindly, "John, you will never be happy until you get your standing right with God."

I've knocked on the wrong door, I thought. "Mable, go in there and bring John a Bible," Ernie said. He was a member of a group called the Gideons, who I knew distributed Bibles and quietly shared what is in it. Mable came in with a whole case of Bibles. Ernie handed one to me and suggested I start reading the New Testament.

I went home, showered and shaved, then went up 15 floors to the office. Opening the book to the New Testament, I began reading in Matthew. While now I know the first chapter of Matthew outlines the genealogy of Christ, a beautiful and careful compilation by God's chosen people, at that time it was entirely meaningless. So-and-so begat so-and-so. I placed the Bible on the desk and began my day. Ernie saw something in that book I didn't see.

12. God's Hand

At 10:30 that morning I had an appointment with a woman whose sister had been killed in an automobile accident and I was to interview her for the defense. She was Black from the town of Helena, Arkansas, wore a modest dress, and carried a tattered handbag. She had a kindly demeanor, a nice smile, and seemed very much at peace with herself in what might have been a somber situation. "Are you reading that book?" she said, pointing to the Bible.

"I started it this morning," I said, ready to drop the subject.

"How did you like it?" she pursued. I told her I started in the book of Matthew, but the genealogy got me off to a slow start.

"You're not very happy, are you?" she said. I was taken off guard, being the one who was to do the questioning.

I said, "Look around. Why would you say I'm not happy?" The expensive décor and view of the Capitol through floor-to-ceiling glass walls didn't impress her.

"It shows on your face," she said.

She opened the tattered purse, took out a little New Testament I later found had been given her niece in the seventh grade by the Helena Gideons. "You need to start with the book of John, then the rest will make more sense." She began to mark in the book and handed it to me. "I've marked some verses. Read them first, then read the book of John." Then she left. I can't recall our interview. Could it be coincidence that two people had given me scriptures on the same day, with the same advice? Everything would change for me with a relationship with God?

At the First Baptist Church in Fort Smith, I had heard some sermons as I sat in the pews with my buddies. Even walked down the aisle with my buddies and joined the church like they did. I had attended a Baptist college and had seen how really devout young Christians were genuine and concerned for others. I believed there was a God, but none of that had been enough to change who I was or what I found to be important in my life. What more did I have to know to enter this "relationship" everyone was telling me about? And I knew if I started into this venture, I would have to find other reliable evidence supporting what the Bible and people were telling me. But I had to restore my relationship with my family first.

13. Life Changes

I decided to read the Bible every morning at work and to leave my office in time to be at home by six each evening. On the first day, getting home at six, I was met at the back door by my daughter Kerry, who had just turned five. She said, "What are you doing here?"

I said, "I live here."

She said, "Well, come on in."

The family was at the dinner table, and I realized my chair wasn't kept at the table but at a desk at the end of the kitchen where Berdell kept the family books. I moved the chair over to the table, retrieved my dinner from the oven, and joined a loving family. We ate quietly.

Every evening when I came in at six, I had to move my chair back to the table, get my dinner out of the oven, and join the family. But after about a month, I came in and found my chair and dinner plate at the table. We had a wonderful evening, and I was sure I was at the place I should have been all those years. At the end of the day, Berdell quietly asked, "John, have you lost your job?" I assured her I hadn't, but that I was reading the Bible and wanted change in my life. She cried and whispered, "Thank you, Lord."

14. The Beginning

Early one morning, reading the Bible at work, I decided I had to have some evidence that what I was reading was true. Paul had said there was ample evidence in the world that God was the designer and creator of all things. That fact had been evident to me since childhood, walking the beautiful countryside in Greenwood, and confirmed many times as I studied the sciences. Today, most astrophysicists concede there is too much evidence to deny a designer of the universe. Most of those also believe that God was both designer and creator. Yet there are some who concede there was a designer, but don't connect it to God, or at least to a God who created all things and who could communicate with created man.

What I find most unlikely to believe is that the designer was capable of designing a universe like ours, yet incapable of creating it. What we know for sure is that God created everything as He chose to do it and when.

For those still struggling with the question, I invite the reading of two books by noted astrophysicist Dr. Hugh

Ross: The *Fingerprint of God*, Promise Publishing Company, Orange California; and *Creation and Time*, NavPress Publishing Group, Colorado Springs, Colorado.

I found it stunning that a scientist could believe that a divine being could create us, the world, the universe, and everything we can see, and yet not be able to communicate with His created beings. Certainly, the overwhelming evidence is that such a marvelous creator would find it quite easy to communicate with us. The God step was easy for me.

Next, I had to come face to face with the issue that God has a perfect sense of justice that required our sins to exact a penalty. The apostle John had said we were all like men on death row, condemned because we had broken the laws of God, which He had made known to us. That God had a perfect sense of justice, and a penalty must be paid for our stubborn refusal to live as God had intended. That the only thing that would outweigh the sins of us all, past, present, and future, was the sacrificial death of His perfect son, Jesus Christ. This wiped clean the slate of our sin and allowed God to forgive us. John said God was motivated by love, as our creator, and didn't want us to suffer the consequences of our sin.

We not only have forgiveness. The apostle Paul said forgiveness of our sins is accompanied by a new life: "If any man be in Christ, he is a new creation. Old things are passed away, and behold all things become new" (II Corinthians 5:17).

I thought about "Uncle Charlie," my beloved grandfather—how his life fit the verse perfectly. A rowdy drunk who became a respected lawman sitting on row four of the First Baptist Church, who, instead of fighting in a bar, fought for justice and helped the lowliest of men and women who wound up in the Sebastian County jail. He would tell them about Jesus in the kindest of ways.

I glanced over to the beautiful sculpture on my desk of "Lady Justice," a stately woman wearing a blindfold and holding scales in her right hand and a sword in her left. Such a figure, which stands in many law offices, has been handed down through ancient Roman and English history, depicting the purity and power of justice. The blindfold indicates that true justice is blind to the power or standing of those appearing before her, and the sword affirms that justice is capable of upholding its decisions. It struck me that if man has for centuries needed justice for an ordered society, why would it be difficult to believe that God also had that perfect sense of justice mirrored in us?

15. Legal Research

While I was certain there was a God and that He has a perfect sense of justice, I needed to know whether Jesus was who He said He was, whether He was telling the truth that He was the Son of God. To believe that a man, dead for three days, was raised from the dead to become the savior of the world was, at best, unbelievable. Yet that belief is the cornerstone of Christianity, and a hurdle that must be crossed if one is to be all in with Christ.

I began reading everything I could find that I regarded as intelligently written and backed by evidence.

An example: Walter Chandler was a premier legal researcher at the turn of the 20th century who had set about to determine if the gospel narratives were reliable enough historically to be admitted in court, under strict rules of evidence. He decided the best way to accomplish this was to write a brief on the subject, and he wrote the book *The Trial of Jesus*. It's pure genius. Written in 1908, it's been reprinted three times, the last in 1972. I challenge any lawyer to read the book and still be unconvinced that Jesus was who He said He was. The proof is overwhelming.

Another example: Simon Greenleaf was the Royal Professor of Law at Harvard and author of *A Treatise on the Law of Evidence*, generally considered the greatest single authority on evidence and used as a textbook in prominent law schools. In later writings, he concluded that the resurrection of Christ was one of the best supported events in history, according to the laws of legal evidence administered in courts of justice.

C. S. Lewis was an Oxford professor, scholar, author, and atheist who set out to disprove the claims of Jesus. By the time he finished his research, he was convinced Jesus was indeed the son of God, and his many books, including *Mere Christianity*, are amazingly clear and convincing. These were just a few of the compelling writers who led me into a full and confident belief that indeed Christ was the answer I had been searching for, and the one who had died for all mankind.

My faith was greatly increased in later years by reading Lee Strobel's books *A Case for Christ* and *A Case for Easter*.

An avowed atheist, Strobel obtained a degree in journalism, followed by a masters in law from Yale Law School, and became legal editor at the *Chicago Tribune*, doing investigative writing. His wife became a devoted follower of Christ, causing him to turn his investigative writing skills to the questions central to Christianity. Was Jesus the son of God? Was he the only person in all of history to be resurrected from three days in the grave? Did his death cover the penalty of man's sins? Is God able to have a relationship with man? What about miracles? Strobel answered these questions amazingly and convincingly. He became an "all-in" believer, dedicating his life to presenting the claims of Christ to the world with more than 20 books and as a teaching pastor and television host.

Early one cool autumn morning, after my Bible reading in the office, I poured out my heart to God, asking that Jesus' death on the cross count for me. I was ready to go all in and let God direct every part of my life, leaving old things in the past and looking forward to better things.

16. Renewal

The desire to be the father and husband I should have always been was now strong, and I begged God to deepen my love for my family and them for me. Besides coming home at six each evening, I announced I wouldn't work on Saturdays and that Saturday morning I would fix breakfast for everyone. I promised I would spend the day doing whatever they wanted to do. Berdell opted to sleep in, a luxury she hadn't enjoyed in the past. After breakfast I gave the kids their choice of what they might want to do. After choosing parks and attending games, they settled on walking to the lake in the woods near our home, sitting on the rocks, feeding the ducks, and listening to stories I made up. Later, my son told me it wasn't until we were face to face and talking that we became a family. They still remember all the old stories I made up. Berdell and I fully restored our love for each other because of her great patience and persistent prayer.

One of my great regrets is that I wasted so much of my life before finding peace with God. But a quote from a recent book, *In Christ Alone*, compiled by Gerrit Dawson, marvelous pastor of First Presbyterian Church of Baton Rouge, has eased my burden in this matter:

> In the book of Joel, the LORD made a promise through the prophet, "I will restore to you the years that the swarming locusts have eaten" (Joel 2:25). When we first get relocated with Christ, we may suddenly become aware of how much we had been missing. It may seem that years spent in self-pursuits left so much waste. So many opportunities to love, wasted. But the miracle of the new creation is that the Triune God makes up for lost years. Being made new in Christ recovers much that was squandered. Even our sins become useful in His mission. The sufferings of earlier years become testimonies to His mercy. When we have let go of our grip on life that we never owned anyway, God gives us more than we could have ever hoped.

God has blessed my family and allowed me to see all my children and grandchildren become followers of Christ.

A family together. Wendy, Berdell, John, Jeff, and Kerry

17. CBMC

With my newfound faith, I was encouraged to join Christian Business Men's Committee (CBMC), which conducts weekly Bible studies for men. It also sponsors quarterly lunch meetings with an invited speaker who gives a testimony about his conversion to Christ with guests who may not have a Christian walk. It was designed to encourage men that their relationship with Christ is the key to being successful in all parts of their lives. Giving such a testimony came easy for me as my whole life had changed. My business relationships and my family life were sources of joy, and being able to share my story, often with frustrated businessmen, resulted in several lives being changed.

I was invited to be the speaker at the Houston Texas Mayor's Prayer Breakfast, sponsored by CBMC, which a very prominent Houston law firm helped organize, inviting many judges and lawyers to attend with other businessmen and women. I was feeling fine about the invitation until I was given the list of those who had spoken before me at this event. Tom Landry had been one of them. It was too late to back out. How would this Texas crowd respond to a lawyer from Arkansas they had never heard of?

Speaking at the Houston, Texas Mayor's Prayer Breakfast. Thirteen judges make a decision to follow Christ.

The convention center was full when I arrived. The mayor introduced me, and I began with my usual attempt at humor at a breakfast: "You've had a good dose of cholesterol this morning. My dream in life is that my doctor will tell me my oat bran level is too high, and I need to eat more bacon and eggs." I presented my life before and after Christ, as you have read, and closed by leading anyone who needed a life change to pray silently as I voiced a model prayer. A response card had been left at each chair, with a place to indicate if they had prayed with me or if they wanted to learn more about CBMC where they could know about a new life in Christ. The response was more than I could have imagined.

Among those who prayed with me, and signed a card of commitment accepting Christ as savior, were 13 judges. I was able to follow up with all 13, many of whom had dramatic salvation experiences. Many lawyers and other men and women also responded. I realized for the first time that God could use us beyond our capabilities if we trusted the Holy Spirit's lead. I decided I would take on tasks that were beyond what I could do alone, and that was the beginning of amazing things.

I was invited to give my testimony in many major cities.

18. Dave Parr

One of the men I had met at CBMC meetings was Dave Parr, one of the most dynamic men I have ever known. Dave was a neighbor who had organized the milk producers in Arkansas into a powerful lobbying force. He later organized milk producers all over America, allowing them to become a powerful lobby in Washington, D.C. Dave had a way about him that demanded one's attention. He had become so powerful that he became entangled in the Watergate investigation and had gone to federal prison rather than "rat" on others. God had no part in his life.

In prison, his job was to make pies. He had gone from one of the most powerful men in America to prison pie maker. He was asked to join a prison Bible study group and he reluctantly agreed. From my experience in doing Bible studies in jails and prisons, I can say when that steel door slams, even the most powerful men look for answers. Dave joined the group and became just as ardent a Christian as he was a worldly power. When he was released, he came back to Little Rock, joined CBMC, and fearlessly confronted businessmen with his testimony about man's need for Christ.

He was the quiet force behind many successful fundraisers for the homeless and needy. He would come by my office and say, "We're having a fish fry for Friendly Chapel. I'm leaving 50 tickets with you, and I'll come by on Wednesday and pick up the money." Brother Paul Holderfield, pastor of Friendly Chapel Church, confirms that Dave's salvation was the perfect picture of how a man's life changes when he allows Christ to take first place.

Early in my conversion, after a CBMC meeting, Dave asked if I had a morning prayer time at home. I told him I had what I called my Interstate 40 prayer on the way to work. I didn't tell him that the morning before, on my way to work and in the middle of prayer, a guy had pulled in front of me, and I had interrupted the prayer to call the guy a bad name. It turned out to be Dave Parr.

Dave put his big hand on my shoulder with a grip, and said, "If you don't have a morning prayer time, you'll never reach the potential God has for you." And added, "and at the end of it, raise your right hand and say, 'today, I want to volunteer for whatever You have for me to do in Your kingdom.'" Dave also was key when CBMC started the Governor's Prayer Breakfast in Little Rock, one of the most successful in the country.

19. The Gideons

Because my salvation experience had come about from reading a New Testament distributed by the Gideons, I was asked to relate my story at Gideon events around the state at pastors' banquets and other local Gideon "camp" gatherings to encourage the Gideons in their lay ministry. I learned that Gideons International was founded in 1899 by three traveling salesmen who wanted to furnish Bibles to hotels for guests at no cost. They expanded the distribution of Bibles and New Testaments to other places where people might have a chance to read them. And it was all for the sole purpose of presenting the gospel of Christ.

They had floundered at first, but the local Ministerial Alliance asked to join in their efforts by allowing their churches to help with purchasing Bibles, and pastors would recommend men who had a heart for sharing the gospel. From there, the mission spread based on some sound principles: they promised God that every contribution to the Gideons by churches and others would be used only for the purchase and distribution of scriptures, and that any expenses would be covered by small dues charged to join or by Gideons willing to travel at their own expense. And since they came from almost every denomination, they wouldn't be talking about doctrine or politics in their meetings. They wanted their sole reason for existing to be sharing gospel of Jesus Christ.

These principles drew me to the ministry. I recognized that reading the Bible alone is sufficient to bring us to God, having experienced that myself. And I was impressed they continued to use all contributions as promised. I found men and women in the Gideons to be humble servants, not needing praise or recognition. And it was in the Gideons that I saw more opportunities to use the power available through the Holy Spirit to see marvelous things take place. Today, the Gideons place millions of scriptures each year in over 200 countries in 109 languages, with more than 270,000 men and women involved in the effort. Recently, the Gideons distributed their 2.5 billionth scripture.

I had found the Gideons to be right in the center of what God was doing to introduce people to Christ, so I eagerly joined and started working in my local camp. New members are appointed to camp offices, and I started as Camp Chaplain. The men and women were faithful to hand out free scriptures to schools, hotels, hospitals and doctor's offices, military induction centers, and jails and prisons, and were willing to share a word of testimony when the opportunity arose.

At a state convention, I was given the opportunity to serve as State Chaplain, and later as State President. I was giving my testimony in events around the state, all while maintaining my law practice, but I had a growing concern about continuing to juggle both work and ministry, knowing both were essential. One morning, I came across these words from the Sermon on the Mount:

"Therefore, I say unto you, take no thought for your life, what you shall eat, or what you shall drink; nor yet for your body, what you shall put on. Is not life more than meat, and the body than clothes? Behold the fowls of the air: for they sow not, neither do they reap, nor gather into barns: yet your heavenly Father feeds them. Are you not much better than they?" (Matthew 6:25-26).

And these words: "for your father knows that you have need of all these things. But seek you first the kingdom of God, and His righteousness, and all these things shall be added unto you" (Matthew 6:32-33).

I left my office and headed for my pastor's office, Bible in hand. When I arrived, he greeted me and asked what he could do for me. "What's the kingdom of God?" I asked. He looked a bit confused. "What do you mean?" he asked.

I said, "Look here in Matthew. It says, 'Seek you first the *kingdom of God*, and His righteousness, and all these things will be added unto you.' So, what is the kingdom of God?"

He smiled, opened two books, studied a moment, and said, "It's the reign of Christ in the hearts of men."

I said, "So, He wants me to seek first the reign of Christ in the hearts of men, and He'll give me the time for my work, too."

The pastor smiled and said, "Yes. He'll give you the time to do both. And don't forget to stay in a right position with Him. That's part of the promise."

Later that day, sitting on a beautiful hill at a park overlooking the city, I thought about what the pastor and the Bible had said, and then out loud said, "God, I'm going to take You at Your word. My goal for each day will be to do my work well and tell someone about You. And I'm not going to worry about it anymore."

20. Teresa

The goals at Gideon state conventions are to urge men and women to share the gospel, to teach them how to do it, to show how a local camp should function, and to contribute to the Faith Fund, which goes to foreign countries that struggle to raise their own scripture money. In my second year as State President, we had a goal of $125,000 for the Faith Fund and raised $150,000. Conventions begin Friday at noon and conclude on Sunday morning, with the Gideons meeting early for prayer then fanning out to do church services. At the conclusion of our prayer time, a Gideon from a small town walked in, obviously teary-eyed.

He told us that he was in charge of hiring a young woman to babysit with children of Gideons during the convention. She was a young girl, 16, who went to his church and was present every time the doors were open. She lived with her grandfather because her parents were drug addicts somewhere in California. They lived in a small mobile home in Greenwood. The Gideon said he paid her $60 for the three days of the convention, and while taking her home, she asked, "What do the Gideons do with the Faith Fund?" He told her, "We buy scriptures for people in other countries who can't afford to buy their own. Young people like you and others."

He said, "She gave back the envelope with the $60 in it, and said, 'Here, I want to give this to the Faith Fund.'" He handed me the envelope. This was a very poor young girl who could have found many ways to spend her money. I was thankful for her heart, but almost sad she had given the money back.

The word got out in the camps about what Teresa had done. I started getting money in envelopes, "For Teresa." Several thousand dollars came in. Then we got word that Teresa's grandfather was very ill and not expected to live, and Teresa was apparently in distress over what to do. On a trip to California, I told her story at a meeting of the Gideons, and after it was over, a doctor and his wife wanted to talk about her. They had no children and said they would be happy to have Teresa come and live with them. They also would contribute to her college expenses. Teresa is now a college graduate and in full-time service to the Lord.

21. Africa

Early in my work with the Gideons, I was invited to join a group of other men from around the world to go to Tanzania and Zimbabwe, Africa, for a Bible Blitz. Twenty-two American Gideons would meet eight men from other countries where we would join local Gideons who found it difficult and expensive to make distributions by themselves in the bush schools in those countries. It was there I encountered men and women who pray and expect God to answer.

My first assignment in Tanzania was to meet a young man in Arusha, near the foot of Mount Kilimanjaro for distributions into the jungle schools. When he arrived at our meeting place, a local store, he was driving a pickup truck with the name "Heifer Project International" on the side. Little did he know that Heifer started in Arkansas, and the international headquarters is in Little Rock. The driver was a 27-year-old Maassai named Simon, a very handsome young man who still bore the markings of his tribe. He was a Christian and a member of the local Gideon camp, had

The only photo I have of Simon (in the middle behind me)

been raised in the area, and knew the location of the jungle schools. I was to find out later he was a celebrity in many of the villages for having helped them develop a herd through Heifer. We had a prayer time where he asked God to keep our truck moving.

"Jump up in the back," he said. "The front seat is full of boxes." I hopped in the back, stood behind the cab, and grabbed the roll bar. Roads in that area are partially paved and one lane. If a vehicle approached from the opposite direction, just before a head-on collision, both drivers move to their right three or four feet. That meant the cars would pass with inches between them, and never slow down during the passing. My grip on the roll bar was for dear life.

By the time we got to the jungle roads, which were dirt, the speed dropped to a crawl necessitated by the deep ruts and ridges of the mucky clay. I was to discover the reason for Simon's prayer, "God, please keep our truck moving."

We would bog down in ruts three feet deep, and at times, come to a stop for lack of traction. I later learned that Simon had never driven a car or truck, having had only a non-moving lesson from his supervisor. I was glad I didn't have that information while gripping the roll bar and meeting oncoming traffic.

When the truck would stick, there would be silence, and almost immediately three or four men would come out of the bush and push us out. Simon would wave to them and move on. After a few miles, I could hear singing, and soon there were students running along beside us. "They know the Gideons are coming," he would shout, and the young girls were carrying boxes of scriptures on their heads from the storage room nearby to the courtyard of the school. "Before we meet with the students, we'll join the headmaster and the faculty for tea inside." The entire

Simon's prayer, "Lord, help keep our truck moving" was a good one.

school had gathered for this occasion, and I thought how different they were from our schools in America.

Inside the school, the faculty sat, mostly women in brightly colored smocks and head-dresses, while the headmaster ceremoniously thanked us for coming and told us what an honor it was. The tea was heavy with goat's milk, and I had a hard time getting it down, but I knew it would disappoint my hosts if I didn't drink it all. So I decided to chug-a-lug it and hope it stayed down. My decision to drink it quickly wasn't one of my best. The headmaster had assigned a young female student to refill our cups as soon as we had finished the first ones, and she took the assignment seriously.

"There is a large rock in the courtyard, with steps carved out of it," the headmaster said. "When you step to the top of the rock, the students will get quiet and listen to what you have to say." As I stepped to the top of the rock, I felt a bit guilty that I was the one who had this in-

African students listen to the gospel story.

credible privilege. I had been in the Gideons barely two years, while the men in my home camp in North Little Rock had been serving in it much longer. They had quietly stood on school sidewalks to hand passing students a copy of God's word. They had called pastors for the opportunity to speak in churches as a report to their congregations about the work of the Gideons. Yet I was the one stepping up on the rock. While I hadn't prepared a formal address for the students, I knew exactly what I needed to say.

I had heard my fellow members speak to students when they had the rare opportunity to do so in Arkansas schools before they had been stopped from doing so. "This book is a love letter from God to you and me," they would say. "It says that God made us and loves us, but we all have turned our backs on God's love from time to time and gone our own way. Because God has a perfect sense of justice, we can't disobey Him and get off freely. But because He loves us so much, He sent His son Jesus from heaven to pay the price for us by dying on a cross. All we have to do is accept this gift and follow Him." I carefully spoke these words to 300 young African students as they sat quietly in front of me.

"You will notice the name of the book we gave you is New Testament. It tells us how God guarantees what He says in the book is true and makes a promise to us that if we will give our lives to Him, we can share His joy and peace. And when we die, we will join Him in heaven. On the first inside page is a place for you to write your name. That means the book belongs to you. If you turn to the very back you will see how to accept God's gift. And if you decide to accept Him, there is another line for you to sign. That means you belong to Him."

Simon and I watched as the students read carefully, but eagerly, and many began to write their names in the back. He talked to the students about how to speak to God in prayer and to listen as He speaks to us. He told them how important it was for them to read the whole book and follow what it says to do. He also gave some of his own experiences, how he always knew there was a god and how a missionary had showed him the true God. And he finished by telling them how he had been blessed as he followed God in his daily life.

Leaving that first school, Simon told me that most of the students had never held a bound book. Most of their textbooks were pages stapled together, and that was why they held out their cupped hands when handed a book. They regarded it as holy. Many of the schools followed the

"I finally got one of my own."

Many students signed the back of their books.

pattern of the first, and we saw hundreds of students write their names in the back of their books.

The Tanzania experience created in me a passion for seeing young people come to Christ, and the knowledge that when we are doing God's work we can, through faith, see His hand at work in supernatural ways. We need only have the courage to ask for what we need and step out in action to see it come about.

On my last evening in Tanzania, I was able to spend some time with Simon, something I now believe God ordained to teach me about dedication and confidence in His power. I knew he wasn't married and asked if he had someone special in his life. He told me he was very much in love, but that it was customary for him to give some cows and goats to the father of the bride. He was two cows short and saving his money. I offered him enough to buy two cows and he turned me down. I got the impression he would not have wanted to substitute my providing it instead of trusting God to do it.

It occurred to me, since he hadn't driven before our adventure, to ask how the scriptures had gotten up to the schools before we arrived. He explained how he had built a large wooden pull-cart and loaded it with boxes of New Testaments, pulling it up the mountain roads. "How long did it take you?" I asked.

"Only a few weeks," he said, as if it were nothing.

"Did you get paid for doing that?" I inquired, knowing the answer as soon as I asked it.

"No," he said. I asked why he would take so much time off without pay at a time when he was saving his money to marry, and why he wouldn't take my offer for cow money. He said something about knowing men were lost without the Christ and wanting it to cost him something for what he did, hauling the scriptures to the schools.

Our Gideon group handed out 165,626 scriptures to 454 schools and eight hospitals in Tanzania.

Leaving Tanzania, we arrived in Harare, Zimbabwe, on a Friday evening where we met the local Gideons. They were people of great faith, and we learned amazing lessons from them. We recounted some of the problems we had in Tanzania where some headmasters had refused to allow us to give scriptures to the students. I was now going to see how people of great faith deal with barriers.

The Camp President said, "We're going to get on our knees and pray for two hours that God will allow us to get into all the schools." There were 360 schools on the list. I had never prayed for two hours, especially not for one request. I had experienced God's hand at work, but this was a big prayer.

At the end of two hours, everyone stood and the president said, "Okay, that takes care of that." Little did I know, it really did take care of that. It was Friday night and we were to begin school distributions on Monday morning. In the meantime, I was assigned to have the full service at Saint Paul United Methodist Church on Sunday morning. A local Gideon, a dentist I had met on Friday night, picked me up for a ride to church. I noticed he drove slowly, timing every light so it was unnecessary to apply the brakes.

"I need new brakes," he confessed, "but spares take a year and I have to make do for six more months." The economy in Zimbabwe was in tatters under a dictator president, and land was being confiscated for those in power.

The church was a beautiful old cathedral style, and 888 people filled it. It was the 75th anniversary of the church, and a cake replica was placed in the front, with two women cutting small pieces as each member came forward to receive one. The pastor was gracious, giving a warm welcome to the Gideons with a kind introduction. I began my church presentation with a personal testimony of what my life was like before I followed Christ and what it was like having Him in my life. How God had transformed my relationship with my family and given me a reason to live. How living with Christ as the head changes all things. Then I told the congregation about our plan to distribute scriptures in the schools and asked that they pray we could get into all of them. At the conclusion, I invited anyone who would like to ask Christ into their life to come forward.

From the very back came a tall, very well-dressed man, kneeling at the front, weeping. I knelt down beside him with a hand on his shoulder, waiting to see if I could help him. Then he stood up, taller than me, and introduced himself. He was the assistant minister of education in

Harare. If we had trouble getting into any school, we should tell them Mr. Molife said it was okay. If they needed to, they could give him a call. He gave me his card with his personal phone number. We got into every school.

In all, we distributed 345,626 scriptures in 814 schools, 13 hospitals, and one college on the Tanzania/Zimbabwe trip.

The Africa trip had been an inspiration, seeing how God worked even in the midst of great injustices suffered by many African people. Those in power seemed oblivious to the misery of the poor, helping only themselves. That situation haunted me long after I returned home.

22. The Legislature

One morning, after reading in the newspaper about an injustice involving a piece of legislation passed by the Arkansas legislature that greatly favored those with significant wealth, I remembered a vow I had made as a college student.

As we had sat at the feet of Dr. Bob Riley at Ouachita, he impressed on all of us our responsibility for public service. He had served in the legislature in Arkansas and regarded that and his military service as payment for living in a free country. He said democracy needed constant care held together by willing service. He had given up his sight in that service. Later he would serve as lieutenant governor of Arkansas. I remember he said that public service must be done with a passion to make life better for those you represent. I could see the need for people in government to remain clear of special interests and simply seek to make life better for those who didn't have life as good as I did. I vowed to take on that task if I ever had the opportunity.

I decided it was time to pray about running for office. It wasn't as though I had spare time with my law practice, and work with the Gideons was keeping me busy, but doors started opening, which I believe is one way God makes His will known to us.

A friend who had represented my district in the House of Representatives was stepping down. The district was Pulaski and Perry counties, a large and diverse area. The head of a large transportation union with 2,500 local members had filed for the position, as well as a woman I knew very well who was a successful realtor. Two other men I didn't know at all signed up, and I paid the filing fee and jumped in.

It was a hard-fought race with honorable opponents who ran on the issues rather than against each other. I ended up in a run-off with the union head and was fortunate to win. He later went on to head the national union and has been my friend for many years.

The Arkansas House of Representatives was led by its Speaker of the House assisted by the Parliamentarian who had held the position for years and was apparently the only one who knew all of the house rules, a combination of *Roberts Rules of Order* and more than a hundred years of "other rules." Studying the rule book at home, I was frustrated, unable to make sense of it for practical use. I was accustomed to knowing the law when confronted with a situation. But help was on the way.

Berdell created a "wheel-chart" consisting of a large cardboard wheel containing all the possible motions in the book, with smaller concentric wheels containing all the responses to the motions. They were interlocked in the center with a brad. It was a thing of beauty. I would need it in the first session.

The most senior member introduced a bill that would effectively engineer a takeover of my city's electric department by the largest supplier in the capital city. He obviously intended to take advantage of my inexperience and help a lobbyist friend. When he made the motion to advance the bill, I quickly consulted the wheel and found a response, then stood and asked the Speaker if I could be recognized. I then made a motion that would effectively table the bill for the rest of that year. The bill's sponsor was shocked. "Can he do that?" he asked the Parliamentarian.

"Yes, he can" was the reply. The wheel remained a help during my entire tenure.

Later in my first session, the senator for my district said he had passed a bill in the Senate that would place our city, North Little Rock, back in the State Library system. Our former mayor, during a dispute, had taken the city out of the system, costing the city several thousand dollars a year. Two other cities were also being added. The bill would be coming over to the House side, and he wanted me to make certain it passed in the House. He said it would be attached to one of John Miller's regular finance bills, all of which came up late in the afternoon. "It should be no problem," he added.

When the bill came up, a representative from a small town stood and objected, "This is one of those big city bills. Let's vote it down." I was surprised, not realizing there was a rivalry between the larger and smaller cities. It was voted down. Needless to say, the senator was unhappy. "What happened?" he asked. I explained that Tom Collier had opposed the bill. He said he would come back the next afternoon and get Tom out of the chamber for the vote.

The next day the senator called Tom out, but he would only move to the back door of the House, keeping an eye on the proceedings. When the bill came up, he shouted, "It's that big city bill," and it was again defeated. John Miller informed us that he needed to get the main bill passed and would give us one more chance to get ours through.

At this point, it's necessary to point out that the house had a "no smoking" rule, but Tom Collier chewed tobacco and used an old Folgers coffee can to spit in. As the time drew near for the bill to be presented, I noticed that Tom was in his chair but leaning over to talk to the guy next to him. I quietly moved over, reached under his desk and retrieved the Folgers can, hiding it in the men's room. I told

The governor signs the bill concerning the State Library System. Behind him with me are Senators Cliff Hoofman and Max Howell.

John Miller to wait until I gave him a signal to bring up the bill. Tom developed a mouthful, looked for his can and left the chamber in distress. I signaled John, and the bill passed.

The next day I got a call from the local civics teacher asking if I would come to her class and speak on "How a Bill Becomes Law." I thought of the old saying, "There are two things you don't want to watch being made: sausage and laws." I shouldn't have done it, given the House of Representatives needs to have the respect of the public, but I gave the class both the official version, and the real-life one. Tom Collier, now a good friend, enjoyed the laugh when I told him.

The governor, Bill Clinton, asked if I would agree to sponsor his legislation along with another member of the House. We developed a friendship. It was then that CBMC wanted to start a Governor's Prayer Breakfast in Little Rock, and the governor was a great help. Many well-known speakers were invited in to come and give a Christian testimony. Governor Clinton would always appear and welcome the crowd. At the end, businessmen and women were invited to join the speaker in a prayer asking Christ into their lives. Many found a new life by attending.

I am often asked about former President Clinton by those curious about him. I believe he had a sincere desire to help the people of our state, especially those who needed help the most. I'm disappointed in his failures, but Christ said I am not the judge of others. Besides, I have my own failures, like the rest of us.

After spending six years in the Arkansas legislature while practicing law, I was asked by the governor to take an appointment as a judge of a circuit court in Little Rock, a court of unlimited general jurisdiction. I would earn less, but would have more control of my time. I was hesitant. I had gone into the legislature with the notion that I could change things for the better for the good people of Arkansas. That notion had grown increasingly dim as I worked my way through the legislative process. The final blow came when a woman who worked in the basement offices of the Capitol asked me to come down and see the conditions in which she was forced to work. As we opened the door to the offices, one could hardly see the office workers for the dense smoke.

Workers were allowed to smoke at their desks, and those with allergies were told to "get over it." I introduced a bill that would require all state-owned buildings to provide a smoke-free workplace. The bill would go before the health committee.

Legislative committees consist of 20 people. A majority vote was required to move a bill out of committee and onto the House floor for a vote. Fifteen members promised they would support my bill. The Surgeon General had recently reported that second-hand smoke was as damaging as direct and gave astonishing statistics as to the death rate for smokers. I produced several leading physicians who supported the bill to testify at the committee hearing. No one testified against it.

When the vote was taken, the bill failed. Many of those who promised to support the bill voted against it. When leaving the room, I confronted one of those who had reneged on a promise.

I said, "You promised to vote for my bill and voted against it. How could you do that?"

He smiled and said, "We just couldn't vote against George." George, not his real name, was the lobbyist for the tobacco industry.

I said, "But you went back on a promise. Does that not mean anything?"

He said, "John, you just take this job too seriously." I decided I needed take the judgeship.

23. Judge Digby

Two weeks before my first day on the bench, I got a call from the judge who had presided for 24 years over the court to which I was assigned. He asked if he could come to my office and talk about some things. This judge was a Sunday School teacher at my church and was loved and respected by the whole community. When he came in, he said, "Have a seat."

I said, "Okay, this sounds serious."

He said, "John, if you'll get on your knees every morning before court and ask God for wisdom, you'll find joy in this work. If you don't, you'll mess it up, and that won't make me happy." Wow. He wanted to be sure I didn't mess up the court he had worked so hard to be a standard of justice.

"I will, judge, I will."

24. On the Bench

The county was restoring the 100-year-old courthouse, and I was given a budget to furnish the courtroom. I hired a bailiff who was a fine young Christian man who suggested that his country church was building a new building, with new pews, and that the old oak pews, 14 feet long, would be perfect for seating in the courtroom. Only one problem: they had a cross carved into each end. We decided to use them, hoping we would have no complaints, and had a prayer service dedicating the courtroom and pews, and specifically asking God to let justice prevail in all things.

Our staff of young Christians made things go well. I had formed a morning habit of praying, then raising my right hand and saying, "Lord, today I want to volunteer for whatever you have for me to do in your kingdom." For the next 14 years, God would allow remarkable things to happen, and while people of all walks of life came through that courtroom, we never had a complaint about the pews. They remain 27 years later.

One of my primary observations through the years of law practice was that we are endowed with a sense of right and wrong that exists outside of the laws passed to ensure we do right. Sam Laser had called them the "unwritten laws" that come to light in some cases and were more sacred to jurors than the written law. Lawyers needed to be aware of them and their importance.

Before I became a Christian, I wasn't sure where those unwritten laws came from. I had thought they must have come from God, but was unsure since some people didn't seem to observe or obey them. I assumed that those who don't probably didn't start out that way—that maybe their circumstances or a series of bad choices had seared or obliterated that treasured gift. When my early search for God had shown He had a perfect sense of justice, I knew they were from Him. We just have a choice to accept or reject them. I needed to keep this in mind on the bench.

One of my earliest cases brought home the truth of Sam Laser's observation. Two men came to court, one accusing the other of breaking his nose. Both men were big, but the one with the broken nose was much bigger. Both men drove trucks for different companies that supplied concrete for large construction sites and occasionally their paths crossed. The bigger man, the plaintiff, had been dating the smaller man's ex-wife for two years, and over that time when they met, the bigger man made sexual references about how the ex-wife enjoyed him more than her ex-husband. And over the years, the smaller man had refused to bite and ignored the comments.

But one morning, the big guy repeated his rants, and the smaller man broke the big guy's nose, knocking him down.

The lawsuit followed. The facts were undisputed with the big man admitting to his bragging and the smaller man admitting he had punched him. After hearing the testimony, the jury quickly returned a verdict for the defendant.

After the trial, in my chambers, the lawyer for the big man said, "I know my guy shouldn't have said those things, but that didn't entitle the defendant to break his nose."

Always trying to think before speaking, and failing on this occasion, I said, "Sure it did. One thing lawyers should figure out is that there are unwritten rules that are far more important to people than some of our written ones. Some of those rules are about decency. For example, you don't talk about the relations you are having with a man's ex-wife. It'll get your nose broken, and a jury will ignore the law that says words don't justify an assault." It's called jury nullification, a recognized legal facit.

The lawyer wasn't convinced. I went on to say there is implanted in most of us a sense of what is fair and right, and what is unfair and wrong. I gave the example of being on a highway when traffic from two lanes on the freeway is required to merge into one. I asked him, "How do we merge two lanes?"

He quickly responded, "One car from each lane, alternating."

I asked, "Where is that rule written down?"

We agreed there are countless unwritten rules we all know about. The lawyer asked, "Where does this sense of justice come from?"

I said, "From God himself."

25. International Challenge

Busy on the bench and still serving as president of the Arkansas Gideons, I attended an International Gideon Convention in Indianapolis, Indiana. On the third day, I was asked to meet with the International President, who said he had prayed about it and wanted me to join the International Extension Committee, Area Nine, and supervise 14 Asian countries in my spare time. I would need to travel to countries including Burma, Sri Lanka, Philippines, Malaysia, Korea, Pakistan, Oman, and others. I was completely stunned by the suggestion. I almost laughed at first, but composed myself and asked if I could pray about it.

"You have about four hours," he said.

As I left the building, things were flying through my head. I probably shouldn't have done all the volunteering after praying, I thought. Looking for a church to pray in, I found a Catholic church across the street, entered the empty sanctuary, and lay face down in the back of the church. I thought of five good reasons why I couldn't do this crazy thing. I had bought 33 acres of land and was making large monthly payments on it. I had a family to support. I had one of the busiest courts in the state. I still had Arkansas Gideon responsibilities, and I was involved in my church. I remember saying, "God, I have never asked You for a sign, but if You want me to do this, You're going to have to give me one."

I was due to go downtown where the Gideons had erected a platform where men and women would give testimonies, encouraging downtown listeners to ask God into their lives. I was to give a testimony. On the way, I decided my five good reasons were adequate to refuse the offer. When I approached the platform, I saw a surgeon on the stage, a Gideon, who a year before had accepted a Gideon assignment in South America. I had wondered how an active surgeon from New York could possibly manage the time and travel schedule required to oversee a foreign area.

I introduced myself, not telling him about the assignment I'd been asked to take, and struck up a conversation. I finally asked him, "I know you took an assignment to Area 3. Can you tell me what went through your head? I know you're not retired."

He said, "John, I had five good reasons why I couldn't take that assignment, but God took care of every one of them." Wow.

Thinking about Simon and the other African Gideons who had no fear of taking on huge assignments and trusting God for the outcome, I decided it was time for me to do something I couldn't possibly do alone. It was time for God to keep His word in the Sermon on the Mount. I would go back to the hotel see how Berdell felt, hoping she would agree.

On the way, I remembered a conversation we'd had a few years before about a worry of hers. At first, she had appreciated my joining the Gideons, thinking it would bring me closer to the Lord. But when I had gotten so involved, she had expressed concern my deep involvement was sending us down different paths. We had talked for several hours, but in the end, I had said I felt strongly that God had led me into this work, and I needed to stay with it. And she agreed I must.

Years later, she told a group of women in the Gideons that after this conversation, she decided to get active with me and had prayed, "Lord, if You want me to join in, You're going to have to make me like it." She went on to become State President and loved the women in our home camp, around the state, and later those from around the world.

Entering our hotel room, I asked her to sit down, I had something I wanted to present to her. I told her what I had been asked to do, including being gone up to six weeks a year visiting camps in 13 Asian countries. She didn't say anything at first, then started laughing, loudly. "Why are you laughing?" I asked.

"John," she said, suppressing another laugh, "you get lost going to the grocery store. How are you going to find your way home from Pakistan?"

26. God's Promise

After returning home we wondered how God would work out my five good reasons for turning down the assignment. He wouldn't disappoint.

Two days later I got a call from Berdell's parents, who lived in Pine Bluff, Arkansas. Bert had worked for Arkansas Power and Light for 40 years and missed three-and-a-half days' work. Millie had a huge garden and canned all they needed to eat. They had gone through the Depression, and their frugality was world famous. She always ate off of the children's menu when we travelled because it was cheaper. They honored God with their lives, doing what was right, and always generous with folks in need. And they were tithers. Bert asked if I would come to Pine Bluff the following day and have lunch with them. When I got there, they had lunch on the table, and a brown paper sack next to my plate.

After lunch, Bert said, "John, we heard about your new assignment, and Millie and I know you have a lot going on, so we wanted you to have this." The sack was sealed, so I thanked them and left.

After driving a few blocks, I pulled over and opened the sack. In it was $35,000. I could swear I just heard the Lord say, "Got anything else you think I can't handle?" I never had to use one cent of that gift, but it was clear to me that I couldn't raise enough barriers that God couldn't overcome.

The following day I got another call from Judge Tom Digby. That day, he sat in my office for a different reason. "John, I've heard you are taking on a big responsibility with the Gideons. They're one of my favorite ministries. I know you'll need to be gone some, so I'm volunteering to sit for you whenever or as often as you need me. And besides, the lawyers like me better."

God had just answered another of my five reasons. Judge Digby suggested I adopt a policy in the court that I wouldn't grant continuances except for a very narrow set of circumstances. "You will need to keep your court docket clean." I agreed. Later I would see the wisdom in that advice.

The statistic that judges were most concerned with was how many cases assigned to them were two years old and older. By adopting this policy, Third Division Circuit Court enjoyed the lowest percentage of those types of cases than any of the 16 other courts in Little Rock during my years on the bench.

After Judge Digby had ended my biggest problem of being gone from the bench, God just as easily removed all the others. As he had promised, if we seek first the kingdom of God (the reign of Christ in the hearts of men), He would take care of all our needs. As my friend Brother Paul would say, "Sometimes God just shows out."

27. Asia

My first trip plans were much too ambitious. Ten days in Sri Lanka, 10 days in Burma (now Myanmar), and eight days in the Philippines. I would later know that two weeks was a maximum for being 13 time zones away and still being fit to hold court when I returned. But in that first trip, hard as it was, God clearly showed me we can't understand His power until we're unafraid to take risks for Him. To go all in—to trust Him regardless of what we're facing. That He is a mighty God, capable of handling every situation.

When I first began traveling in 1989, planning trips into Third-World countries was difficult. Although Gideons are businessmen, that definition in other countries is broader than in the United States, and many have little resources. Counting on them to meet me when I arrive and help with transportation was tenuous at most. What I can say is that those men taught me about sacrifice, tenacity, faith, and devotion to God's work.

The excitement of my first assignment trip kept me from sleeping the night before I was to leave Little Rock and land, 22 hours later, in Colombo, Sri Lanka, off the coast of India. The country had been in a civil war for 15 years pitting the Tamil Tigers in the north and east against the Sinhalese, the majority population that controlled two-thirds of the island. The Tamils made up around 15 percent of the population occupying the northern city of Jaffna and the eastern city of Batticaloa. Preventing the annihilation of the minority was the fact that millions of Tamils were on the mainland of India and might retaliate in the event of an all-out war.

I was told I couldn't visit either of the Tamil-controlled cities even though we had Gideon camps there. They had not been visited in several years. But three days before my trip, a ceasefire was announced, so I planned to attempt visits to those cities as well as Kandy in the central part of the island.

Landing in Colombo at 4:30 in the morning, I was met by four of the local Gideons excited to get the day started. The trip into the city was eye-opening. Some roads were lined with cardboard shelters where people cooked and slept, and the smells of food cooking were jarring to the extreme. All this within sight of modern buildings and wealthy business people, seemingly oblivious to the poverty, much like some cities in my own country.

The Gideons had planned an early training session, distributions to schools and prisons, and the presentation of a dignitary Gideon Bible to a government official. At noon we were to have a luncheon in the home of one of the Gideons. The women of the Auxiliary wore beautifully colorful dresses, genteel in every respect. But when we gathered to eat, there was no silverware. I watched as the hostess began to eat with her fingers as did everyone, and I could only follow what was the obvious custom. The food was so spicy hot, I was unable to get much of it down. I lost 15 pounds in this 28-day trip. I should have learned about local diets.

The Colombo Sri Lanka camp

From Colombo on the coast, I traveled inland to Kandy by train. The beauty of the island was breathtaking, and inland the island is basically a mountain range. Most of the population lives on the coastline while the mountain interior is sparsely populated with rice farmers and a few small merchants who reminded me of the country stores in Arkansas.

I was warmly received by the Gideons in Kandy, and after meeting with my Christian brothers and sisters, I was ready to take advantage of the ceasefire and attempt to visit Batticaloa. Unfortunately, the locals in Kandy didn't trust the ceasefire and nobody wanted to travel east with me.

I was directed to a young man in his mid-20s who had a car rental business. I attempted to rent one of his old and well-worn vehicles, and asked if he'd drive me to Batticaloa. At first, he refused, saying he had never been on the east side of the island, that nobody he knew had been there because it was considered too dangerous. I informed him of the ceasefire, and he laughed. "Those happen a lot. You can't depend on them."

I said, "How old are you?"

He said, "Twenty-six."

I said, "Don't you think it's time you saw the other side of your own homeland?"

He thought a moment and said, "Maybe it is. Let's go."

We started out at eight in the morning traveling unbelievably rutted roads, but seeing the most remarkable mountainous beauty. The tiered rice fields looked like huge steps going up the mountainsides and were dotted with oxen pulling plows guided by lone farmers who stopped in amazement at our car passing by. Apparently, no traffic came from Kandy and only local folks used the narrow roads. Rounding a curve, we suddenly passed under a waterfall that poured completely over the road. When we emerged, beside us was a family taking a community shower. They were shocked to see us. Truly, I was on a trip experienced by few people.

Nine hours later as we neared Batticaloa, we rounded a curve to find a huge log blocking the road. Men with AK-47s stood beside it and motioned for us to stop. My driver told me to stay in the car and say nothing. He got out, walked up to the men, and began a lengthy conversation. I prayed. The men would point at me in the car, and there was much discussion. After an eternity, the men moved the log and we were allowed to pass.

When we were safely by, I had to ask what the discussion was all about. He told me the men wanted to know who I was, and he had told them I was a missionary. He said, "If they had known you were a judge, we'd have been in trouble."

Arriving at the gates of Batticaloa at just after five, we found that the Tamils had closed the city to all entering traffic. I was devastated, knowing the Gideons of Batticaloa hadn't been visited in several years, and thinking the arduous trip accomplished nothing. But the young driver had been impressed at what he called our "valiant effort" and was

My brave guide who traveled to the other side of his country for the first time.

proud to have been to the other side of his homeland. I gave him a New Testament and a brief testimony. We arrived back at Kandy at two in the morning. Only God knows why things happen as they do. It may have all been for the young man to know Christ. I was able to contact the Gideons in Batticaloa by phone. They appreciated our efforts.

Following Sri Lanka I landed in Rangoon, Burma, now known as Yangon Myanmar, and was ushered to a desk in the airport where an official demanded 300 American dollars in exchange for kyats, the local currency. I wouldn't be permitted beyond the desk until I paid. "Our kyats are equal to your dollars," the man said. Having prepared for unexpected expenses I made the exchange.

I was met by "Sonny" in a late-model van. He was a Gideon who headed the Rangoon YMCA, a position of great importance in that culture. The military government, feared by the 50 million inhabitants, had refused to recognize a democratic election and ruled with an iron hand. Sonny was allowed great latitude to operate the three-story building, renting rooms to locals needing a place to stay and working with young people. He also was head of the local Gideon camp. I was to discover he was a true diplomat who knew how to get along with the worst of dictators. There was no international phone service out of Burma at the time, something I had warned Berdell about. We would be out of contact for 10 days.

Burma is mostly Buddhist with a much smaller Muslim population. Christianity is allowed to exist so long as it doesn't attract attention. I was scheduled to stay in Rangoon five days, travel by plane to Mandalay for three days, and return to Rangoon for two more days. Sonny had planned every minute of my stay in both cities. I have learned that God has His people strategically placed around the world, dedicated to His will. It is a comfort to know these people are just where they are needed.

I had sent letters to the eight camps scattered in the country of 260,000 square miles, telling them my schedule and inviting those who could to join me in either of the two cities I would visit. The purpose of my visit was to encourage these men and women, help train them in the ministry, and teach them how it is best carried out. I had no idea how many could manage the journey across the vast country. I would be surprised. I was also to meet with a local printer who printed our Burmese scriptures. Gideons attempt to have as many scriptures as possible printed locally to help the local economies.

On my first morning, Sonny had arranged for me to have breakfast with a local "ambassador," and Sonny would join us with a couple of local Gideons. This was my second encounter with a culture of eating with the fingers, and so I was prepared to eat like a pro.

What I hadn't planned is for others to curiously reach over and handle my food to see what was between the two pieces of toast Sonny had place in front of me. Little did I know that would be the least discomforting of my dining experiences in that part of the world.

The "ambassador" sat across from me, and with a heavy accent, said what I thought was, "I want to go to America, and I wonder if you could help me with my etiquette?" I'm thinking, first I'll tell him about eating with forks and spoons.

"Well of course, I'd be happy to do that." With that, the ambassador rose to his feet, raised both arms, and shouted, "Oh, praise God, praise God." His response was so surprising I had to rethink quickly what he had just said, and what I had just agreed to do.

"Did he say etiquette?" I asked.

Sonny had a big grin on his face. "He said, 'air ticket.' Not etiquette. So nice of you to help." Then Sonny explained my error, and we all got a big laugh. For the rest of the trip I listened more carefully to what people had to say.

Sonny (in the tie) and the Rangoon camp.

28. Beautiful Feet

After breakfast, the local Gideons began to gather in our meeting room, and Sonny introduced each one as they came in. While most were members of the local camp, some had come from adjoining villages and others from far away. They were delightful men who had been able to take part in the distribution of scriptures in that country, thanks to the support of the Gideons and Christians in other countries.

Mid-morning, there was a knock on our meeting room door, and Sonny opened it to a very tired-looking man. His feet were dirty and his worn leather thongs were caked with red clay. I thought they might be the ugliest feet I had ever seen. But his smile was as broad as his face as he proudly announced, "I'm Laurence Aung, and I'm from the Baseen camp." Sonny put his arms around the man and hugged him.

"Welcome back, Laurence," Sonny said, telling me this man was a faithful Gideon from the Baseen camp several hundred miles away. "He has come by riverboat starting several days ago."

Laurence Aung

We offered Laurence some food and tea, and all the men began to ask him about his camp and the work there. I was so flattered to think he had come so far to see me, but Sonny explained that while he was glad to see a man from headquarters, Laurence makes the trip twice a year to pick up boxes of scriptures to take back to his camp for distribution. He was a pharmacist.

When it was time for Laurence to leave, he went to the scripture storeroom at the YMCA, and the little man picked up a huge box of New Testaments to load onto a motorized bicycle Sonny had arranged to get him back to the boat. Scriptures printed in Burma are on thick paper, and their New Testaments are much heavier than those printed in America. When he was ready to go, Laurence came to me and, putting his arms around me, thanked me for being there and the Gideons for supplying the scriptures.

As he got into the seat to go, I looked back at his feet and thought of the scripture in Romans 10:15, "... how beautiful are the feet of them that present the gospel, and bring glad tidings of good things." His feet were no longer ugly. This man, who takes the duty of sharing the gospel seriously, now had the most beautiful feet I had ever seen.

Two experiences in Rangoon have stuck with me. First, the city has many orphanages filled with children whose parents couldn't feed or take care of them. They are beautiful children whose faces bear both the sadness of their experience and the laughter that comes with having someone love them. Their cheeks were decorated with thanaka, a pinkish powder I saw on faces all over that country. Sonny said thanaka was an herb that softened the skin, prevented wrinkles and sunburn, and also kept mosquitos away. We could give the older ones scriptures because they were taught school lessons there. They were kind and affectionate, as were most of the people I met in Burma.

The second experience that stuck with me from Rangoon was coming across a roadblock for road construction and looking down a wide dirt street where adults were hauling large rocks up to a group of young children who were on their knees, breaking the rocks into small pieces used as gravel to cover the dirt road.

"Why aren't these children in school?" I asked. Sonny explained that very few children had the privilege of school, mostly those from wealthy parents. My heart sank. Breaking rocks was a penalty in many prisons of the world, and these children had done nothing but be born in the wrong place.

When it was time to move from Rangoon to Mandalay, I was taken to the airport, taking comfort in having bought

Rangoon orphans

Rangoon students

tickets in advance in the United States. I had heard I should be prepared for many travel barriers in Burma. When I presented my ticket, the same man at the desk informed me that the ticket I had purchased for $300 was "no good" and I needed to buy a new one. I proudly pulled out the kyats I was given on arrival and plunked them down on the desk.

The man was livid. "You can't use these," he said.

"But you told me they were the same as dollars. That's all I'm going to pay." I was bluffing, but to my surprise he took the kyats and handed me a new ticket.

Arriving in Mandalay, I was met by a local Gideon at the airport who took me to the Silver Cloud Hotel, third floor. It was surprisingly clean and, while appearing to have been built by the British years ago, had been well kept. From my window I saw a landscape dotted by beautiful Buddhist Temples, their golden domes shining in the sunlight. I found the people to be hard working and polite. They would take a scripture and promise to read it.

Training the local Gideons how to distribute scriptures and lead others to a knowledge of Christ was a pleasure. They were diligent and eager to learn. I was given the privilege of speaking in a local Protestant church and found it packed with godly people wanting to hear what God was doing in the world through the Gideon ministry. The stay in Mandalay was a delight, and I felt honored to be there. But I had run out of Hershey kisses and was losing weight fast, unable to eat most of the fire-hot local food. Also, I had fussed at the Lord because my knee hurt. It was like, "Here I am serving you, so why don't you do something about my knee?"

Returning to Rangoon for the night, I was taken the next morning to the airport for departure to Bangkok, Thailand. The same uniformed agent who had extracted 300 American dollars on my arrival was there to greet me, but I pulled out an empty pocket and walked by him quickly for my gate to Bangkok. It's discouraging that since my visit to Burma, their movement toward another democratic government has failed miserably.

The last leg of this 28-day trip was welcomed. I had lost 12 pounds in 20 days, had diarrhea since leaving Sri Lanka, and hadn't been able to talk to Berdell for the last 10 days. Looking at my itinerary, I had flights from Rangoon to Bangkok to Manilla, where I would spend the night. Then from Manilla to Davao City as International Representative to the National Gideon Convention of the Philippines.

In Manila, my good friend Lawrence Ti met me at the airport and handed me his new cell phone to call home. Berdell was glad to hear from me, and I was missing her terribly. Before taking me to his home for the night, he asked, "Do you like pizza?" Then he took me to a local place where I devoured an American-style pizza that warmed my empty stomach. Sleep was welcomed. The 13-hour time difference I had been working in was taking a heavy toll.

Lawrence took me to the airport the next morning where I departed for Davao City and the Philippine convention.

29. Davao

Davao City is a beachfront paradise with beautiful waterfront cabanas, quite a contrast from the last 20 days. We had a very spiritual meeting with the hundreds of Gideons and Auxiliary members who had come from many different islands of the Philippines. Quite hard to imagine that Davao is where missionaries were held hostage by rebels a few years later.

A thousand Gideons had come to Davao to celebrate another year of serving God by distributing His word and sharing a testimony with lost people. My assignment, as the international representative, was to let them know what God was doing in the ministry in other countries, to train them in being more efficient, and to inspire them with testimonies about men and women who were sharing the gospel with great sacrifice. By the end of the convention, I was the one who was inspired by the people of the Philippines.

There are 5,000 islands in the country, and God's people there are an amazing testimony to devotion and courage.

The plane trip from Davao back to Manilla for my journey home was one I will never forget. Having checked my luggage straight to the U.S., I got on the plane with just my briefcase that contained a small bag with toiletries and some handkerchiefs. I had grown accustomed to the practice on local flights that nobody honored the request to stay seated until the plane reached the gate. As soon as the plane neared the landing area in Manilla, people began to stand and open the overhead storage areas. Often, bags and other articles fell out, so in self-defense it was wise to stand with them for fear of getting cracked on the head with something.

Standing as the plane landed, we struck the ground with such force that many were knocked to the floor. My knees had buckled, but I had managed to stay upright. Fearing the worst, I looked down and saw I had ruined my pants. The plane came to a halt, and I was a mess. Wondering what I could do since I had no other clothes, I slipped into the bathroom of the plane and shut the door as people moved forward.

I had never felt so absolutely lost for a plan and wanted desperately to get to the international airport a few blocks away and go home. I glanced in the small mirror of the plane, and I looked awful, smelled terrible, and just felt crushed. As I looked in the mirror I said in a loud voice, "Why, Lord, why?"

I had never experienced an audible voice from the Lord, and not sure this one was, but as clearly as a loud voice, the Lord said, "John, I never promised this journey would be easy. Only that I would be with you, and I am here."

I had never before, and haven't since, experienced such amazing warmth mixed with sheer joy. I took off my pants, stuck them in the small sink and washed them as best I could. The Thompson's Wonder Pants I had been wearing were still very wet but I put them back on and sloshed out of the plane. My bags had been moved to the international airport for the flight home, so I ran the few blocks to the terminal, worried I was going to be late for my flight.

When I got to the gate, the attendant said the flight was leaving. But, as I had grown accustomed, a uniformed man said, "Sir, follow me. I'm going to get you on that flight." He pounded on the door of the plane, and it opened. There was one seat left on the front row, and I sloshed to it, all eyes on me and my wet pants. Unmoved by the predicament, I had never felt so close the Lord and enjoyed a wonderful flight home. I'm not sure if those seated around me could say the same.

Gone for 28 days on the other side of the world, and a time difference of 13 hours, my internal time clock was upside down. At night I was wide-eyed and sleepless. When daylight came, I was fighting sleep like crazy, not looking forward to holding court. Fortunately, I got a call from Debbie, my efficient case coordinator, telling me my case for the next day had been settled. I was able to get a bit more accustomed to the time difference before holding court, and I had two months before traveling again.

Berdell had done her amazing job of taking care of everything at home, and we were happy to have time with each other.

30. Getting Healed

Two weeks after returning home, I got a call from Carol Smaley, head of the Oasis Renewal Center in Little Rock, one of God's best places for people who need help of all kinds. Battered, handicapped, down-and-out, and addicted people find renewal and a relationship with Christ. Carol asked if I would speak to the handicapped group. "They're amazing people who will lift you up more than you can lift them. But they still need encouragement."

The large rustic log dining hall was filled with young people, many in wheelchairs, all smiling and talking as if they had no handicap at all. The first young man I encountered was in a wheelchair with only finger-like arms, but with a huge smile. He was probably 18. I was shocked to see how happy he and the others were.

Carol stood up and said, "Okay, let's have prayer requests."

Several people made requests, and then back in the middle of the group a young woman stood. She was less than five feet tall, and her head was so disfigured it took my breath away. Her face was very long and narrow with eyes that looked as if they had been reconstructed by a doctor to help her looks. She had been born blind.

She had a beautiful smile and said, "I don't have a prayer request, I have a praise. When I was trying to learn to walk without sight, I always felt like I was going to step into a deep hole. But God is good, and I got over that. But last year I learned I had breast cancer, and I felt like I was going to step in that deep hole again. But God is good, and I'm not afraid of that anymore."

Carol Smaley led a prayer, then said, "Now we're going to sing 'Amazing Grace,' and Carol Ann, you sing that third verse like you always do."

When the third verse came, the small blind woman stood and with a clear and beautiful voice sang, "Through many dangers toils and snares I have already come. 'Twas grace that brought me safe thus far, and grace will lead me home."

I slipped out the back door for a minute and apologized to God for complaining about my knee in Burma. And I thanked Him for the health I had. I guess that's how some Christians get healed.

31. Death Row

Before my next assignment, I got a call from the chaplain of the Arkansas State Penitentiary. They had executed a man recently, and the chaplain wanted me to speak to the inmates on death row who were demoralized after the recent execution. I had met the chaplain when I spoke in his church for the Gideons, and he thought a Christian judge might find a way to reach them. I had never faced the challenge of encouraging men who were facing death, some for unspeakable crimes, living in small cells never to see the light of day again.

As a judge, my docket didn't include criminal offenses, as I had arranged with another judge, an ex-prosecutor, to take my criminal cases and I would take his civil docket. Having never sentenced anyone to death, I had little understanding of the minds of such men. Since my conversion, I had spoken to many different groups, presenting the gospel message as a layman, but this challenge was daunting. I couldn't get an inspiration for a message, even as late as the night before. I was completely at a loss as to what I could say to stir these men to know the peace that comes with forgiveness.

On the evening before, I was watching the Billy Graham Crusade broadcast, and as usual, a testimony was given before Billy spoke. That night it was a stirring message by Dave Dravecky, a champion major league pitcher, who, with a few teammates, preferred to hold Bible studies while on the road rather than party as many of his team members did.

Dave was a lefthander, pitching for the San Francisco Giants in 1989, when he developed a cancer in his pitching arm. After surgery he continued to pitch, but in a pivotal game, his arm snapped, and in that instant he lost not only his baseball career, but eventually his left arm.

As he spoke on the stage at the crusade, his message was based on II Corinthians 4:16-18:

> Therefore, we do not lose heart. Though outwardly we are wasting away, yet inwardly we are being renewed day by day. For our light and momentary troubles are achieving for us an eternal glory that far outweighs them all. So, we fix our eyes not on what is seen, but on what is unseen. For what is seen is temporary, but what is unseen is eternal.

Dave emphasized that those words were spoken by a man who was later executed on death row.

I was amazed at how plainly the Holy Spirit had spoken to me and given a clear message for the next day's assignment. Death row consisted of a pod of single cells, two levels high, all of them in a semicircle facing the same direction so that a speaker could see each man as they stood looking through bars. Before I spoke, each man, one at a time, was allowed to be shackled and leave his cell to come down and see his friend, the chaplain. I won't forget how each man, wrists chained, reached over the head of the chaplain to be hugged by him. Tears were shed. I was seeing death row from an entirely different perspective. After each man was escorted back to his cell it was time for me to speak.

I was introduced as a judge, but the chaplain was kind enough to tell them I had never sentenced a man to prison, preferring to be able to speak to inmates rather than sentence them. He told them I was the International Chaplain of the Gideons whose only mission was to present the claims of Jesus Christ. I hoped that had softened the blow of my being a part of the legal system.

One of the men was sentenced to die in a few weeks, and others were facing death at some point in the future. I told them I had a message from a man named Paul, himself a death row inmate, who had written part of the Bible and was sentenced to die because of his religious beliefs. He had been a killer of Christians before having a dramatic experience that caused him to see the truth, and he became a dynamic follower of Jesus Christ.

I explained that Paul, the prisoner who had been promised eternal life in Christ, sang songs because he knew that though his body was dying, his inner man, his soul, was actually becoming greater. And he declared that the concrete walls and iron bars would one day be gone, but that he would be alive in Christ forever. I explained how each of them could also know eternal life by accepting the gift that Christ had given them by dying on the cross to pay the penalty for their sins. Whatever they had done could be forgiven by Christ.

I asked, "What would you think about a man on death row, lying on a gurney about to have the needle stuck in his arm, when the warden walks in and says, 'Hold everything. There's a man outside who is willing to die for you. He will take your punishment and your bad record.' Would the prisoner say 'No thanks?'"

To refuse the same gift from Christ would be just as foolish. Many on death row trusted Christ that night.

32. JACK

Before I left, the chaplain wanted me to meet a young man in a different part of the prison, "the hole" where incorrigible prisoners were held. The chaplain led me down some long steps in the lowest part of the prison, but stopped at the bottom and said, "I want to tell you about Jack.

"Jack is 28 and looks just like all the images you've seen of Jesus. Great-looking young man, but he will only be in shorts and his arms and legs are covered with two-inch scars. His mother and grandmother were witches and would cut him during their rituals. He grew up hating Satan and being in trouble.

"He escaped prison in Louisiana, and a guard was injured during the escape. It was night, and he was running through open fields when he heard the dogs coming closer. He remembers lying on the ground and saying, 'Satan, if you'll get me out of this, I'll serve you.' Immediately, the dogs quit barking, and Jack got away, giving credit to Satan. A year later he was caught and returned to prison, an ardent Satan worshiper. He finished that sentence, but ended up in Arkansas for another offense."

The chaplain said Jack ended up in the hole because he caused trouble. In a single cell he had covered the bars from the inside with newspapers so that his cell would be dark all the time and he would be free to worship Satan. The guards said they could feel the evil coming out of the cell and didn't want to pass it.

Hearing about Jack's Satan worship, the chaplain had gone to his cell, pulled all the papers down, and said, "My God is stronger than yours." The chaplain then sat at Jack's cell and read the Bible to him, telling him how Jesus had come to earth and died to cover all sin, including Jack's. That those who believed in Jesus had their sins forgiven.

After many days, Jack put his trust in Jesus, but he told the chaplain he couldn't sleep because the demons still bothered him. The chaplain said, "Well, you still have all those Satan-worshiping things in your room. I'll sack them up and burn them." After all was taken away and destroyed by the chaplain, on his next visit to his cell, Jack had said, "That's the first night's sleep I've had in years."

Meeting Jack was a pure joy. Seeing this young man, covered with the scars of satanic worship, standing in his cell praising God brought further proof of the truth of II Corinthians 5:17: "Therefore, if any man be in Christ, he is a new creation. The old has passed away; behold the new has come." The experience reminded me that all people are candidates to enjoy the magnificent change of life in Christ. Never to be slowed in sharing the news just because their appearance tells me they would not be likely to receive it.

33. Malasia

I am not one to look for miracles, but in my next assignment I experienced how God intervenes in difficult situations. I was to take part in the Malaysia/Singapore joint national convention an hour north of Kuala Lumpur, the capital of Malaysia. This part of the world had always fascinated me. Malaysia is a divided country with half sharing the Malay peninsula with Singapore, and the other half, East Malaysia, sitting across the South China Sea on the island of Borneo. After the convention, I planned to travel from Kuala Lumpur to Borneo for visits to camps along the southeast coast in the state of Sarawak, one of three states there.

Before the convention began, I visited camps on the peninsula with some of the best of men who serve God with enthusiasm. After our meeting, some of them took me to a restaurant where we were seated at a customary round table. No menu was presented. A bowl was placed in front of each man followed by a helping of rice. The waiter then ladled a serving of soup-like food on top of the rice, and each man stirred it and began to eat. I am not a finicky eater, but as I looked down into the bowl, something was moving and I must have had a strange look on my face. I was asked if everything was okay, and I assured them I was fine. This was a pricy meal these men had secured, and there was no way I wasn't going to eat it.

"Lord, I'll put it in my mouth and you keep it down for me," I said to myself. I was able to eat the entire serving as each man watched to see if I liked it. That was not the miracle, but it was very nearly one.

God must have a sense of humor. He wasn't the only one laughing.

When the convention was over, a Gideon gave me a ride to the Kuala Lumpur airport for a flight to Sarawak in Borneo. A traffic delay caused my arrival at the airport to be close to my departure time, and the Gideon didn't know which of the five terminals would be mine. The thought of missing the plane hit me. There was no way to reach the men in Kuching to let them know, and there wouldn't be another flight for two days.

"Just let me out in the middle," I said.

I walked into the nearest terminal, but none of the departure boards were lit. I had a sinking spell and set my bag down to think. To my amazement, a young Chinese man in a business suit walked up and pointed to a counter. "That's your window." I was confused.

"To Kuching?" I asked.

"Yes," he said. I glanced at the window, then quickly looked back to thank him, but he was gone. "How did he know and where did he go?" I said out loud. The promise of God to work in all things is real. Out of five terminals and countless windows, it was the right window to Kuching. Although the woman at the window said the flight had gone, the man beside her said, "Follow me." He led me out on the tarmac, and a rolling stairway was still at the plane door. The plane door was closed, but the man climbed the stairs and banged on it. It opened and by an obvious act of God, I was able to meet the men who would go with me several hundred miles to Gideon camps of Borneo. I had begun to get used to being part of amazing things.

34. Borneo

Borneo has a fascinating history being occupied for centuries by indigenous tribes, the Dayaks, Bawang Assans, and others, some of whom were headhunters. In later times, there was an in-migration of Chinese, who now make up over 50 percent of the population. The indigenous make up only 35 percent and the rest are non-Malaysian. During World War II, the Japanese occupied Borneo, but were met with great opposition by locals and allied forces. At the end of the bloody war, Borneo was ceded back to the British.

Amazingly, thanks to missionaries, the predominant religion among the Malayan Chinese is Christianity. Most of the Gideon camps are composed of very devout Chinese Christians, with a strong desire to see men and women meet the Jesus they know so well. The coastal camps were booming, doing their job of sharing Christ.

In Sibu, an inland city, one of the Gideons there lived near a village built entirely over water as a defense to the headhunters. The water is about six feet deep in that area and the walkways and huts were built using Bilian, a wood that doesn't deteriorate when stuck in water. Though the threat of dangerous tribes was no longer present, many still live in the water villages. It was amazing to see the past come alive as people went back and forth over the walkways that sank almost to the water with each step. I could imagine how things changed when enemy tribes approached.

The boardwalks sink low to the water but work well for the residents.

While in Sibu, one of the tribal Gideons had gotten a rare invitation from a distant relative, a member of the Bawang Assan tribe, to take part in a ceremony the tribe holds each 10 years. These people are of ancient descent and live in longhouses constructed years before. These houses also served as a defense against the headhunters, and each was about 60 yards long housing 10 or so families. There was a long, wide inside hallway, with each family having an inside doorway to individual units. The idea was that 10 families could more easily defend themselves than individually. I was fortunate enough to be able to accompany the Gideon to the event after he had gotten special permission to bring an outsider in.

The ceremony began in late afternoon when relatives were invited to go to each door and taste the food specially prepared by that house for the celebration. By the last door, having eaten 10 different local foods, we were stuffed. But the celebration was just beginning.

All the people came out into the wide hallway where some were dressed in magnificent costumes. At the center was an ancient gong on a low wooden stand that had served their ancestors as a warning when the enemy was nearby. It was obviously very sacred. In the ceremony, it was struck 10 times with the people silently remembering the threat it brought back from the past.

Those in costumes came to the center and engaged in a tribal dance that had been done when the enemy was turned away. One of those who danced was a very old woman who was a child during the last attack on the longhouse. Tears were shed. Obviously, I had been allowed to be part of the ancient past brought into the present.

Ceremonial gong of warning

Ceremonial dance

My time in Borneo saw very active men and women in the Sarawak Gideon camps, and I was able to get a glimpse into the past of the world of water-villages and longhouses. And they now sat in the midst of an advancing city.

35. South America

Before organizing my next trip, I received a call asking if I would consider moving from Asia to South America, an area of 13 countries much closer to my own time zone. While I had learned incredible lessons from the Gideons on the other side of the world, not having to deal with jet lag would work wonders with my trial schedule. Being right-brained, I would need to listen to tapes and immerse myself in the language to pick up basic communication. I certainly wish I had taken Spanish instead of Latin in school.

I'd need to move from three verb tenses in English to 14 in Spanish. Berdell was the consummate language teacher. I told her she had two months to teach me. My first trip would be to Bolivia and Peru. Later to Brazil.

36. Bolivia

Stepping from Asia to Bolivia, I found a dramatic change in people, geography, and history. Bolivia is a landlocked country divided and diverse in many ways, with the Andes mountains making up a third of the country in the west and the lowlands of the Amazon basin in the east. Even the capital of the country is divided, with Sucre the constitutional capital and La Paz the executive capital, or seat of government. Neither is the largest city, that being Santa Cruz. It has five main ethnic groups and 36 indigenous languages. Most speak Spanish, but Guarani, Aymara, and Quechua are among the tribal divisional voices heard. It remains the second poorest country of South America.

To say the least, Bolivia is both fascinating and beautiful to behold. My plan was to visit Andean camps in La Paz, Oruro, Sucre, and Potosi, then move on to Santa Cruz in the Amazon basin. The Andean areas still bear Incan and Spanish influences, and both seem to have impacted religion and customs.

The Gideons in the camps were dedicated and hospitable, eager to learn how to be effective in getting the Christian message to their people. Gideons who had come before me had established camps and left them in good hands. I thought I had prepared for the altitude of Potosi, the highest city in the world, by taking long bicycle runs for several weeks, but found I still got winded climbing three or four steps. I would find out in Peru how the people managed the altitude.

Christianity in La Paz and other parts of the country had exploded. Churches were packed, and the Holy Spirit was moving in the lives of the people. We were free to distribute scriptures in classrooms, hotels, hospitals, police and fire stations, doctor's offices, and along the streets of cities. Evangelical churches were making a difference in the lives of those in the largest cities.

I had finished with the Andean camps and moved on down to Santa Cruz in the Amazon basin. With a population of over two million, Santa Cruz is the country's business center. I met with the local camp members, who had arranged a distribution at a local jail where about 400 prisoners were being held before entering a larger one of 4,000. I asked the men of the camp why we were not giving scriptures to all the men. They said a jail employee had refused that request.

I suggested we try to see the chief of police and see if we could distribute to the larger jail. The chief was glad to meet us and asked, "Why are you only doing the small jail? Those men in the large one need Bibles, too."

We were able to do an effective distribution in the large jail, and when we invited the chief to our meeting that evening, he arrived early and joined the Gideons. He was a strong Christian and encouraged the camp to think bigger when doing God's business.

Chief of Police, Santa Cruz, and new Gideon

When finishing up my business with the Santa Cruz camp, the president of the camp said he had gotten word there were 18 young Christians in Bermejo, Bolivia, who wanted to start a Gideon camp. They said many of the Quechua people were worshiping Satan, and they believed if they had scriptures, those people would worship the true God.

"Where is Bermejo?" I asked.

"On the other side of the Andes, down on the Argentine border about 300 miles." I was depending on local flights and

Gideons for getting around, but I was pretty sure there would be no flights over the Andes. And Bermejo was a small village. "There's a missionary pilot in Santa Cruz who has a single-engine plane, and he's willing to take you to Bermejo. You'll land in a cow pasture that's been cleared, and they're expecting you Wednesday at noon."

Paul was an American who had always known he was to be a missionary pilot. In his late 20s, he was a skilled pilot who had been licensed to fly before being licensed to drive. And he was as devout as he was skilled, having piloted missionaries many times. We loaded the plane with several boxes of scriptures, had a prayer time, and left for Bermejo.

I was looking forward to seeing the Andes by plane, but low-hanging clouds completely covered them. For several hours we enjoyed a wonderful fellowship in the air as he gave me a history of Bolivia. When the Spanish conquered the area and discovered silver in the mountains, they had been ruthless in enslaving the people to work in the silver mines. There was no way to get oxygen deep in the mines, and thousands of people had suffocated.

When they were taken to the surface, the local people often saw on the corpses small albino frogs that were prevalent in the mines. The Spanish, not wanting the people to know the miners had suffocated, told them the frogs were powerful satanic beings that had killed them. From that time, the people had believed frogs had great power, and many villages still had large statues of a frog at the entrance to the village to appease Satan.

After several hours of flying over clouds that obscured the Andes, Paul turned to me and asked, "Do you have people praying for you?" Not a good thing to hear from your pilot, but it occurred to me that, indeed, I did have people praying for me. The Gideons print an annual Prayer Calendar, and each day, there is a Gideon listed that people are praying for. On that day, my name and picture were listed.

"Yes, I do have. Why do you ask?"

"Because in a few minutes we need a hole to open up. We're about to land."

It's easy to pray under those circumstances, and almost immediately, Paul said, "Good, there's the hole." I thought it was a bit too small, but he was happy with it and dropped down, making a smooth landing on the pasture.

Pilot Paul, (left, kneeling) and Bermejo men greeters

Looking over to the side, nine young men and eight young women were waving. Eight of the men were married, and their wives were dressed in the local attire. None of them had a car, so we walked into the town where they had arranged our meeting in a village gathering house. On two tables they had laid out their applications to join the

Gideons, 10 for the men and eight for the women. I looked them over and they were all in order, except it appeared they had been filled out two years earlier. I called over the young man who seemed to be in charge and said, "These all seem to be fine, but why were they filled out two years ago?" I wish I hadn't asked that question as it had obviously embarrassed the young man.

New members of the new Bermejo camp

"We filled these out before we found out it costs $10 to join for the men and $2 for our wives. But we've been saving and now we have it. Here it is. Take it." I would have been happy to pay for them to join, but it would not have been a good thing as they had obviously trusted God to make it happen.

We organized the camp, elected officers, and had a training session so they would know the way scriptures are to be distributed. And how to use the back pages where the scriptures list how one receives Jesus as Savior. It also directs them to find a local Bible-believing church to have support of other believers. I then instructed them how to order scriptures at no cost once they had given out the box of 100 we gave them. "But we need many more that that," we were told. "There are many people in the area that worship Satan."

Noticing they had no car or truck, I asked them how they would deliver them to other villages. "There's an old bus that comes up the road several times a week. We'll load the boxes in the bus and have it done in just a few months."

We had prayer and the new members of the Bermejo Gideon Camp walked us back to the plane. As we were taking off, I looked back just as we left the ground. Eighteen new Gideons were waving good-bye.

I couldn't help but think, "This is a perfect picture of this ministry. What a sight? How long would it have taken them to pay for thousands of scriptures? But they don't have to because God has a plan. We'll send them what they need, paid for by Christians in other countries who are faithful to give. I could have flown back to Santa Cruz without a plane.

Establishing a new camp, especially in an area that has many pagan worshipers, is always a prayer concern. I was later to learn from another Gideon who visited Bermejo that the camp was thriving. They had faithfully distributed in their area.

37. Peru

Peru has one of the longest histories of civilization of any country, dating back to the fourth millennium BCE. The people are as diverse as their history, living through Incan and Spanish rules, and spanning cultures from Machu Pichu to Lima. Both have high levels of human development including upper-middle-income and very poor areas. Amazing visual differences, depending on whether you are in the arid plains of its Pacific coastlands on the entire western and southern borders, the Andes running from north to southeast, or the Amazon rainforest and river basin to the east. It is a magnificent and boundlessly fascinating country.

My plan was to visit camps beginning in the capital city of Lima on the Pacific coast, move to the high Andean city of Cusco, then north to Yurimaguas on the Amazon river. I would experience all levels of altitude and economies, but find great similarity in the warmth and kindness of the people.

Lima was a highly developed and beautiful city of nine million offering every cultural opportunity of any city in the world. We had freedom to share the gospel at all places, and the camps were well organized and furnished their own scriptures. They needed little training, and I was the one who was encouraged by my visit. In Cusco, things were different.

I had experienced some difficulty with the altitude in Potosi, Bolivia, the highest city in the world at over 13,000 feet above sea level, but it was mostly having to rest when walking up steps. Headed to Cusco, at just over 11,000 feet, I didn't anticipate altitude problems. I was about to be surprised. The airport lies in a bowl between Andean mountains, and landing is a lot like dropping from the sky. But that doesn't deter the two million people who visit Cusco each year.

Setting foot in Cusco is like stepping back in time to ancient Peru. Machu Pichu is but a train ride away, and Cusco has its own magnificent Incan ruins. Amazing, gigantic stones weighing several tons each are expertly stacked into place by some unknown, purely magical engineering. The city of over 400,000 appears to be locked in time, yet enjoys every convenience of modern cities.

Local Gideons had arranged a room in a quaint, two-story downtown hotel run by a man in his 70s. I spent my first morning in a local residence with men and women who were jovial and hospitable Christians, and who wanted to know more about sharing Christ with others. I was starting to learn that God's people reflect the same spirit no matter where they are in this world. They wanted to show me some Incan sights in the afternoon, and I did amazingly well with the altitude, stopping only occasionally to catch my breath.

At the hotel, I was given a room at the top of the stairs, just above the owner's room. I crashed into bed and fell immediately to sleep. But at two in the morning, I awoke in a panic. I couldn't breathe and was struggling to get air. I stumbled down the stairs and knocked on the proprietor's door, trying to stay on my feet. He came to the door and seemed to know the source of my distress. "Asiento." Sit down. He produced a large cup, placed some leaves in it, heated water and poured it on the leaves. In a moment he handed me the cup. Almost immediately after drinking the mixture I was able to breathe again.

"What's in the cup?" I asked.

"Coca tea," he responded. He gave me a napkin with several Coca leaves wrapped in it and said, "put these in your coat pocket. When you get in trouble again, heat some water and make tea." I wore the same navy-blue sport coat during the trip, tucking the leaves in my pocket, but didn't need them again. I noticed that almost every man I saw in the Andes was chewing the leaves. And in the Cusco airport, if you order tea you get Coca tea. Coca leaves are, of course, best known for their psychoactive alkaloid, cocaine, but in the form of coca tea they only open the lungs and make the altitude bearable. It enables workers to do normal work in very thin air, a centuries-old remedy.

Finishing my work in Cusco, I rather happily left the Andes and descended into the totally different world of Yurimaguas in the steamy northeastern Peruvian rain forest of the Amazon River. At the confluence of the Huallago and Paranapura rivers, the city is a major commercial center for subsistence and market-oriented farmers and fishermen. It was at the lower end of the economic scale with what seemed like a sparse population scattered along the riverbanks and farms that surrounded the city.

Men of the Yurimagual camp

As I got off the plane, I was greeted by several very young boys with shoeshine boxes wanting to earn a few coins. Needing a shine I stood against the wall as a smiling shine boy lifted my foot to his box and brushed my shoes. I guessed him to be about eight years old, about the age of my grandson, whom I had entertained with an old coin trick making a quarter disappear by blowing on my hand and retrieving it from his ear.

When the shine boy smiled up at me, I took out a coin and made it disappear, then blew on my fist and retrieved it from his ear. He was fascinated by it and I gave him the quarter and a dollar.

Several local Gideons met me, taking me to Leo's Palace Hotel, a misnomer, and we joined the men and women of the camp at a dinner meeting later that evening. The next day, we had scripture distributions at schools around the city, and at each stop, I saw the shine boy mimic my trick by blowing on his fist.

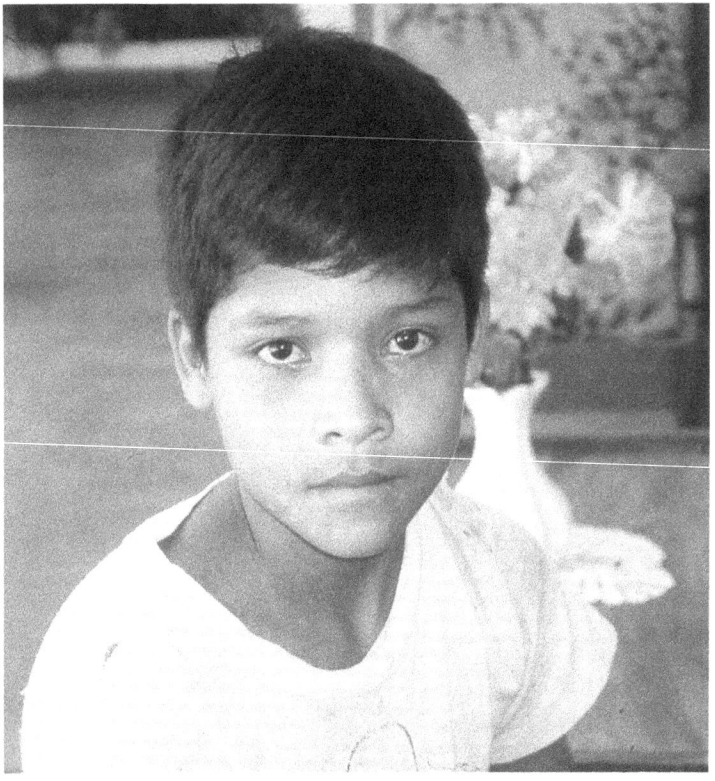

Gonzollo

The next morning, I was to meet a local Gideon on a veranda outside my room. He was right on time, sitting on a bench, as was the shine boy. I told the Gideon about the boy, and he explained that many of the shine boys were living on the streets without parents. He was able to ask the boy about his situation and found out he lived in an empty building taking care of his younger brother. I sat the boy beside me on the bench and asked, "Como te llamas?"

"Gonzollo" he replied. With the help of the local Gideon I asked him what he knew about God, but he was unable to tell me anything he knew.

I explained that God was our heavenly father who created us and wants to know us. "God loves you. Do you know what that means?" I asked. He shook his head. I put my arm around his shoulder and said, "God loves you like this." I'm pretty sure it was the first time Gonzollo had ever been hugged. I took out a little New Testament and explained that God had sent his son Jesus to pay for our sins by dying on the cross. And how Gonzollo could ask Jesus

My new friend and fellow magician Gonzollo

to come into his heart by just asking. I gave him a Testament for his shine box and saw him several more times in the next days as we distributed scriptures in Yurimaguas. My heart ached to know there are many Gonzollos around the world.

38. Brazil

Soon I was to be the International Representative to the National Gideon Convention of Brazil in Iguazu Falls. Three thousand men and women from all parts of the country would come together for fellowship and to share their experiences and learn how to better present Christ to the lost people of Brazil. Many would come from hundreds of miles, taking days for the journey. Iguazu Falls is known for having the largest curtain of falling water in the world. It's on the Iguazu River bordering Argentina, and the beauty of it is indescribable.

My part in the convention would be to speak three times over the four days to the entire assembly, offering testimonies about the inspiring work of men and women in other countries. And information on how to improve their own camp's success and words of encouragement regarding their personal walk with Christ. I would also meet with break-out groups of leaders who inspired me with their devotion to the ministry and to Christ.

On the last night, in my last address to the assembly, I praised them for distributing over five million scriptures to

Iguazu Falls

the lost people in Brazil. After I had spoken, the National President of Brazilian Gideons got up and made an impassioned plea I will never forget. He praised his fellow Gideons, then said of the five million scriptures they had distributed that year, the greater part of that number had been paid for by the Gideons of the United States and other countries. He felt they could do better and suggested they take an offering that would help them cover more of their own Bibles. I was assigned to a group that would count and report what was given.

When all of the bills and coins were counted, there remained in an offering plate two rings. The first was a very small, well-worn woman's wedding band. Some woman in the assembly who probably didn't have money to give had given all she had. I was stunned. I could never part with my wedding band. The other was a man's well-worn graduation ring. I was told it represented graduation from the school of engineering. I now had a long list of things done by people whose devotion to Christ encouraged me. I came home with the rings and donated to the Gideons the value of them, which was small. But in my numerous opportunities to speak at Gideon fundraising efforts I have shown those rings and told their stories, raising money those two people could never have given.

With the Brazilian President

39. Dr. James Thomas

International Conventions of the Gideons, held annually in different states, draw several thousand men and women from all over the world. As many as 70 countries are represented, with seating for each country equipped with earphones connected to interpretation booths, and every word is translated. The International Extension Committee members, those responsible for different areas of the country, invite men from their areas who have a special testimony to present it to the convention. It is a moving and inspirational experience. The Columbus convention was where I met Dr. Thomas.

Dr. James Thomas is on my list of special people who have offered up their lives to God and don't realize they are anything special. He and his wife live in Delhi, India, where he works at a children's hospital as a cardiac surgeon, healing poor children with serious heart problems. When I met him in Columbus, he was serving as President of the Gideons in India. His obvious passions were bringing new life to sick children and bringing new life to those in India who needed to know Jesus as Savior.

He and his wife lived on the campus of the hospital in humble circumstances while carrying out the mission God had given them. They considered it a great privilege, even honored, to be able to serve Christ. We got to know them well at conventions, and they had visited us in Arkansas. We were amazed to learn he had gotten his training as a cardiac surgeon at Children's Hospital in Little Rock.

We received word from him that he and his wife were coming to Little Rock for another visit, and we were always excited to host them. He told me that while he was in Little Rock, he was going to do open-heart surgery on a four-year-old girl and asked if I would like to "scrub up" and watch it. Of course I did.

For five hours, I stood in a frigid operating room and watched a marvelous team perform the surgery. Hardly any words were spoken. Each team member seemed to know exactly what to do and when to do it. The patient looked much younger than her age because her heart had a hole in it that had prevented proper growth. I watched in amazement as her chest was opened and she was placed on the machine that did the work of her heart. The hole was patched beautifully; her heart was placed back into position and began to beat again.

Later I asked Dr. Thomas how everyone seemed to know what to do, as he hadn't worked in Little Rock for years. "I've done 2,500 heart surgeries in India, and had the good fortune of working with this same team while in Little Rock when I was here. You don't forget the protocol." The surgery was done at no cost, as he had donated his services.

I was thinking how simply they lived in India, and said something I now wish I hadn't: "If you lived in America, you would be a very rich man."

His response was, "God didn't call me to be a rich man. He called me to be something better."

40. International Chaplain

After my years on the IEC, traveling in Asia and South America, I attended an International Convention in Indianapolis. We had taken along our 12-year-old granddaughter Erin, who enjoyed the wonderful youth programs and meeting young people from around the world.

I was talking to a Gideon from another country in the lobby of the hotel at the end of the second day when Erin tugged on my coat and said, "Papa, I signed my book." I nodded and, not knowing what she meant, went on with my conversation. Undaunted, she tugged my coat again, "Papa, I signed my book."

I said, "What book, sweetheart?" She held up a little New Testament she had received at the youth service and showed me the back page where she had signed her name to ask Jesus into her heart. Nana and I had been praying for her. We hugged and cried.

Also, at that convention, thinking my international travel days were over, I was surprised to be elected International Chaplain of the Gideons from a slate of good men. No man is worthy of such an honor, representing 270,000 men and women in 200 countries who shun honor only to serve the Lord with diligence and passion. They take seriously the command of Jesus, whose last words on earth were, "Ye shall be my witnesses, both in Jerusalem, Judea, Samaria, and unto the uttermost parts of the earth."

What an incredible ministry, now all over the world because we have only one mission: to share Christ. We don't talk about politics or doctrine. Just about Jesus.

In my time as International Chaplain, God continued to show He is willing to do incredible things all around us when we are confident in His power.

41. Sioux City or Sioux Falls?

One of my assignments as Chaplain was to attend the Iowa State Gideon Convention in Sioux City, Iowa, a trip I will always keep tucked away in my memories of God's goodness. I had a plane change in Kansas City where I was assigned the very back aisle seat. Only one seat was left, right beside me across the aisle. A young man, late 20s, came back to take it. He wore a suit and tie, and was smiling, "Sioux City or Sioux Falls?" he asked.

"Sioux City," I said.

"I'm headed for Sioux Falls," he said. "What's that button on your coat?"

"Oh, that's the Gideons. An organization of Christian businessmen and women."

"Christian? Like, Jesus Christ?" he persisted. I should say at this point that I was trying to keep the conversation between the two of us, but he had a naturally booming voice, and it seemed the whole back of the plane was hearing our conversation.

"Yes, Jesus Christ," I said, 10 decibels lower.

"Well then, I need to talk to you," he boomed. "I was raised a Catholic, but we never went to church. I married a wonderful girl who takes me to the Assembly of God Church, and I can't figure out what in the world those people are doing."

"Well, Sir, you are asking the right person," I said, having spoken in almost every denomination of churches. "Those people are celebrating the great decision they've made to follow Christ with their lives. I can tell you it was the best decision I ever made."

At that point, I gave him my brief testimony. I reached in my jacket pocket and took out a small New Testament the Gideons carry that has some scriptures on the inside back cover that make it easy to see how to make that decision.

"When you get to a quiet place, read those verses. It even has a small prayer you can pray asking Jesus into your life."

"Why can't I do that right here?" he asked. Wow. This young man is determined to get saved whether I want him to or not, I thought.

"Well sure," I said. "Why don't I say a prayer, and you can just repeat it after me?" I bowed my head, put my hand across his arm and quietly said, "Dear God."

He repeated, "Dear God." Four rows up people were turning. I continued the prayer and he followed each line, confessing he was a sinner and asking Jesus to come into his life. By the time we got to the end, he was sobbing.

About that time the plane landed. He stood up, tears still apparent, and said, "I'm getting off here. I'm going to call my wife and tell her what I've done." He headed up the aisle with me behind him.

About halfway up the aisle, a little lady tugged on my jacket and said, "I was praying for you the whole time." I think half the plane must have gotten saved that day.

I lost sight of the young man and went on to the convention. After I spoke to the crowd that evening, recounting my plane experience, a couple came up and asked, "What was that young man's name?" When I told them, they said, "That's our granddaughter's husband."

42. Telling Others

Early in my walk with Christ I was trying to discover my role and responsibility in sharing the gospel message with the world. Turning to the Bible, the answers were unsettling because I couldn't reconcile what I was finding as my responsibility with what I saw among Christians. The Biblical mandate was clear, but so few seemed enlisted in the effort to actually tell lost people about the life-changing gospel. I heard it said, "Personal witnessing is like a football game, 22 participants desperately needing a rest and 50,000 spectators desperately needing exercise." So, I searched the scriptures for the components of sharing Christ. What I found has made the matter simpler and a joy rather than a task.

Many dynamic Christians have their own way of presenting Christ to lost people, and I'm not suggesting anyone should change the method they use as there are many effective ones. But others seem have difficulty finding the words to say. I've heard people say, "Personal witnessing is just not one of my talents." But Christ wouldn't command all of his people to be witnesses if success depended on our talents. For that reason, and for the benefit of those who have left the task to others, here is a clear plan of presenting the claims of Christ. Three things we need to know:

What did Christ COMMAND us to do?
Who are the CANDIDATES (those we witness to)?
And, what is the CONVERSATION we need to have?

43. The Command

Following Christ's resurrection, Mary and other women went to the tomb, only to find Jesus gone. But the angel of the Lord said He isn't here, but He's called a meeting. He wants all of His followers to meet him in Galilee. When Jesus joined them later in Galilee, his last words on earth, found in Acts 1:8, were sure and certain: "But you shall receive power when the Holy Spirit has come upon you; and you SHALL be my witnesses in Jerusalem, in all Judea and Samaria and to the end of the earth."

The COMMAND is, we SHALL be Christ's witnesses. None are exempt. He even told us where to begin. With those around us, (Jerusalem) among family and friends, then outwardly in concentric circles to the ends of the earth. In truth, it seems Christians are doing a better job of reaching the ends of the earth than with those around them, given we have missionaries, Gideons, and other ministries that help us reach the ends of the earth. Family, friends, and acquaintances we meet around us are sometimes more difficult with which to open a spiritual conversation. But they should be first on our list.

Many Christians fear the "imposition" of talking to others about their relationship with God. Perhaps they think they've got to be Bible scholars, able to quote the Roman Road scriptures. Memorizing salvation scriptures is a good thing, but isn't at all necessary to be a successful witness. The disciples didn't have the New Testament, and they built the foundation for the whole world to know Jesus.

In II Corinthians 5:19. the apostle Paul made clear what our role is in this matter of bringing the world to Christ: "That is, that God was in Christ reconciling the world to Himself, not imputing their sins to them, *and has committed to us the WORD of reconciliation*" (my emphasis).

Clearly, the role of the Christian is simply to get the word out. We are NOT responsible for whether the person accepts or rejects Him. Charles Spurgeon, the great English pastor and evangelist, said: "Christ didn't come to make bad men good or to make good men better. He came to make dead men alive." People without Christ are dead with regard to where they will spend eternity and need someone to show them life. We can hardly make their situation worse if we tell them about Jesus.

44. The Candidates

First, we have to know that lost people fall into different stages of readiness. Jesus made that clear in the parable of the sower of seed. In Mark 4, he said there were four groups of people that received the seeds (the word), and three of them were not ready to receive it, for various reasons. But one of the important points Jesus made is that SOME ARE READY NOW. Like the young man I met in the plane to Iowa.

I have definitely met people who were ready and needed very little encouragement to ask Christ into their lives. As we'll see, sometimes others have laid the groundwork, and those who are ready now are the result of their labors. I just wish those who are ready now had PURPLE NOSES. It would make things easier, but if we're in a mindset of looking for opportunities, we'll encounter them.

Of course, those not ready now still need a witness. Another important point Jesus made by the parable of the sower is that even though some are not ready to make a decision, nonetheless the sower included them. In John 4 and I Corinthians 3, we learn that one may sow, another water, and yet another harvest. We haven't failed just because a sinner's prayer wasn't spoken. For one person, you may be preparing the ground. For another, you may be planting the seed of the gospel for someone else to harvest, or you may get to harvest what someone else has labored over. So remember, lost people are either UNPLOWED, UNPLANTED, OR UNHARVESTED. And SOME ARE READY NOW.

I regard the parable of the sower of seed as Jesus' seminar on personal witnessing regarding the CANDIDATES.

And from experience, I can say that if we don't concentrate on one person, we'll be overwhelmed by the need to reach the world. So, think about one person you believe needs to know Christ and write his or her name on a piece of paper. It may be someone you have known for years, a family member, or a newer acquaintance. You'll need to pray that God will allow you to reach the point in your relationship that you will be able to turn the conversation to spiritual matters. It may take time.

As one pastor asked, "Who is your one, and when will they hear from you what matters most to them?"

45. The Conversation

We are told in the Bible that even if we stand before kings, God will give us the words to say when presenting the claims of Christ. For that reason, there is no need to present a script to follow. But as a good place to start, remember that when Jesus sent out the disciples to win the lost, He only asked them to bear witness to what they had SEEN, HEARD, AND EXPERIENCED ABOUT HIM, which would simply be their testimony. We all have a testimony of how our lives went before Jesus, what we did to receive Him, and our lives after we accepted Him. We can look at Jesus' approach to know when the time is right to give it.

First, we need to remember that when He was on earth, most people didn't approach Him by asking how to be saved. They came to Him with problems, illnesses, and other physical needs. By meeting those needs, He gained their trust and faith. And that's how many will come into our lives. God has called us to be servants. Meeting the needs of people like Jesus did is what we are about as Christians. Our motivation is to reflect Christ's love through our service. We will find, as we gain their trust through service, the door opens to introduce them to Jesus. And the door opens widely by asking one powerful question. It's a very non-threatening one, enabling us to offer the real solution to their problems. Here's an example:

A lawyer who came to my chambers was distressed about a problem he was having with his practice. He had lost one of his biggest clients, which seemed to be only one of his concerns. His life wasn't going well in other areas either. We spent several hours during which I was able to offer solutions that could help repair his practice, but his depressed mood persisted. The time was right for the question. I asked, "Do you ever think about spiritual things?"

His answer was, "Well, my wife's a Presbyterian. If I ever get to heaven, it'll be on her ticket." That answer told me a lot about God's place in his life, which is the object of asking the question.

It's difficult for those who have no relationship with God to realize that He is the help for all their relationships. And when all our relationships, including with Him, are healed, all the rest falls into place.

It was the perfect time to give my testimony.

I told him how the goals I had set for my life centered on money and status, but had led to emptiness and a shattered home life. That people who cared about me told me how their relationship with God had changed all their other relationships. By reading the Bible, I realized my need to be forgiven, and that Jesus had paid the price of my sins by dying on the cross. I told him my friends had been right. God was the answer for the changes I had been searching for, and they had changed for the good.

My lawyer friend wasn't ready to make a decision right then, but I could tell he had listened. I had plowed some ground and planted a seed of the gospel. I invited him to attend a meeting of Christian businessmen where he heard other accounts of changed lives. He joined a Bible study and later made his own profession of faith in Jesus.

46. Conversation Barriers

Sometimes those we talk to will put up barriers before they are ready to enter into a conversation about spiritual things. Perhaps they don't trust anyone with what seems to be such a personal matter. They may feel you are intruding in their lives. The Bible's account of how Jesus overcame some of them is helpful.

His intentional encounter with an outsider, a Samaritan woman at Jacob's well, shows how He turned the conversation to spiritual matters.

Jesus left Judea headed north, on His way to Galilee, having a specific person He wanted to encounter that required Him to go where other Jews would never go. Most Jews would go out of their way to avoid Samaria, but Jesus was on a mission and went through Samaria instead of around it. About noon after a long journey on foot, He reached the location of Jacob's well. He stopped there and sent His disciples into town for food. A Samaritan woman came up with her vessel to draw water.

It was customary in the first century for women to fetch water in the coolness of the morning or evening. Never at midday. Perhaps this woman sought to avoid the crowds due to her reputation. Whatever the case, Jesus asked "Will you give me a drink?"

Probably surprised, the woman said, "How is it that you, a Jew, would ask me, a Samaritan woman, for a drink? For Jews have no dealings with Samaritans."

At this point Jesus had ignored both ethnic and cultural barriers. Jews would not share food or a drinking vessel with a Samaritan for fear of ritual contamination, regarding them as racially unclean. And for a man to speak to a strange, unaccompanied woman would be culturally unacceptable for a Jewish man. In doing so, Jesus showed He had no such prejudices.

Having removed those barriers, Jesus then turned the conversation to spiritual matters. He said, "If you knew the gift of God and who it is that asks you for a drink, you would have asked and He would have given you living water."

Realizing this man had brought up a spiritual subject, she put up another barrier, pointing out that He didn't have anything with which to draw water and the well was deep. "So where are you going to get this living water? Are you greater than Jacob who dug this well?"

Undaunted by this attempt to divert the conversation, Jesus turned back to spiritual matters. He told the woman amazing personal things about herself that only the Messiah could have known.

Obviously impressed with all Jesus had said, she finally entered the spiritual conversation. "I know that the Messiah is coming called Christ, and He will tell us all things."

At which time Jesus said, "I that speak to you am he."

From there, the woman left her water jar and ran into town telling the people she had met the Messiah, bringing them back to the well to meet Him. Jesus spoke with them and went back with them to the town, staying two days during which many became believers. Jesus used His One to bring many to Him.

Obviously, we will give a much different testimony than what Jesus gave, but His example is enlightening. When we arrive at the appropriate time to talk to our someone about Jesus, we should keep a singular mind. We should have the courage to present our life before we knew Jesus, what we did to receive Him, and what our life is like knowing Him. The Holy Spirit will be in charge of giving you the right words and convicting our One of sin. It's a beautiful thing to experience. Remember we are only ambassadors of Christ, as though he is speaking through us. And always encourage the new Christian to find a Bible-believing church to have the fellowship of other believers.

47. The Building Contractor

Don't expect everything to go as you planned.

When you start with your prayer asking God to lead you to a person, the Holy Spirit takes over with His own plan. I'll give you an example of what may happen.

Speaking to a graduating class in a town near mine, I ended by encouraging them to allow God to lead their lives. To get on their knees each morning and volunteer for whatever God has for them to do that day.

A young woman came up afterwards and told me she was a follower of Christ, but that her father had never included God in his life. She handed me a card with his name and business address, and asked if I would go talk to him. She explained that he was a successful building contractor and was always busy, but had never been convinced he needed God. She knew that his life had been empty, and he had searched for answers. I promised her I would do my best to meet with him. She asked that I not tell him she requested it.

For a while the card stayed on the desk in my office. I would pass it every time I walked by, but for some reason I put off making the call. One day as I was leaving the office, I knew it was time, so I went back. It was a Friday afternoon about two when I called. I introduced myself and said "I'm with a Christian men's group, and I was wondering if I could come by and speak to you for a few minutes." I was not expecting the call to go well, given his history.

"When did you want to come?" he asked, with a booming voice.

Not wanting to push, I said, "Sometime next week, if that would be good."

"I'll be busy next week. How about this afternoon?" he asked. We set 3:30. God's timing is amazing.

On my way to his office, I thought about how to open the conversation. I'd recently been involved in a large construction case, so I would start talking about that to break the ice. Then I'd find an opportunity to give my testimony. I found his building, but there was no secretary in the front office late on Friday, so I entered the empty reception room and saw a door that looked probable. I knocked and a big voice said, "COME IN."

My knees were wobbly. "Sit down right there," he said, motioning to a large easy chair. He was as big as his voice. I sank almost to the floor, and he was a giant, sitting behind his desk. I was looking up as he said, "Now, what is it?"

I was hoping something would come out if I spoke, and forgetting all about the construction-case ice breaker and my testimony, I blurted out, "Sir, if you died today, would you go to heaven or hell?" I couldn't believe my ears. Did I say that?

He got up, walked toward me, growing as he came nearer, then walked past me and knocked on another door. A small older man opened it and came in. "Earl, do you know what this man just asked me?" he said.

"No, what did he ask."

"Well, he asked if I died today, would I go to heaven or hell?"

"What did you tell him?" the small man asked.

The next thing I know, they are kneeling down in the corner, praying. Tears were being shed.

I left.

Probably three years later, I was speaking in a church in Northwest Arkansas, and when the service ended the music director asked if I would stay around for a few minutes. His wife had been in the choir and wanted to speak to me.

She asked if I recognized her, and I confessed she looked very familiar, but I couldn't recall who she was. She said, "When I graduated from college, you spoke to our class. I asked you to go talk to my father who was lost. His partner had been trying to lead him to Christ for years, but he hadn't been interested. When you went to see him, something happened, and he prayed a sinner's prayer with his partner. I just wanted to thank you for going to see him."

What I realized from that time on is that the Holy Spirit can use whatever effort we put forth to do marvelous things. A willingness to just open our mouths and speak is key. I was prepared to give my testimony, but the Holy Spirit had a plan much better than mine. I've had several such things happen over the years, and it never ceases to amaze me what great power we have in the promise of the Spirit to give us words, and convict of sin. But more often I end up giving my testimony.

48. The IRS Agent

Let me challenge you to start a morning prayer time if you haven't done so already, and at the end of your prayer raise your right hand and volunteer for whatever He has for you that day, and ask that He give you someone to speak to. Then, look for opportunities to take on whatever challenges that are clearly bigger than you are capable of handling on your own.

I have to confess, my failure to be consistent in this challenge has caused me much grief over the years. I tell it so you won't make the same mistake.

One morning after praying for an opportunity to share Christ with someone, I got busy at work in my law office when my secretary came in and said, "There is a man here who says he is from the IRS, but isn't here on business. He wants to see you. He has on a suit and tie, and I think he may have had a drink. He isn't drunk."

Not taking the matter seriously, I said, "Tell him I only see clients by appointment."

She left, but came back and said, "He won't leave. He wants to see you."

I said, "Show him back, I'll get rid of him."

A very well-dressed man in his 40s sat down and introduced himself and, before I could say anything, said, "I work for the IRS, and recently fell at work. I have a head injury, with seizures and have to take pills for it. I'm not supposed to drink while taking the pills, but I haven't been able to stop."

I thought, why in the world is this guy telling me all this stuff? He wasn't drunk, but I needed to get him out of the office.

I said, "Why don't you go get a good physical exam and let the doctor help you?"

He stood up and walked out into the hall to the elevator. I followed him out, feeling badly for not being more concerned about his situation.

As the elevator door opened, he looked back at me and said, "You spoke at a church in Cabot, and the pastor told me if I came to see you, you would help me. But I guess he was wrong." Then he stepped into the elevator and left. Immediately, I remembered my morning prayer. The help he had sought was obviously spiritual, and I blew it.

Two weeks later one of my law partners came in and said, "You know that IRS guy that came to see you? Well, he died Friday."

I was stunned. How could I have missed the man God sent me?

Our morning prayer request for God to bring someone into our path is serious business.

Until God places someone in your path, remember to write down the name of your ONE on a slip of paper and put it in your billfold or purse. And remember, it's a Command, not a suggestion, and the "kingdom of God" is the reign of Christ in the hearts of men. Doing it in your own power is not faith. Faith is obedience, regardless of how things look.

"But without faith it is impossible to please him: for he that cometh to God must believe that he is, and that he is a rewarder of them that diligently seek him" (Hebrews 11:6).

49. God Has a Sense of Humor

Following Jesus produces the life of joy we are intended to live. He makes sure our lives are filled with peace that only He can give, and it includes all kinds experiences. Many are serious, but many will bring fun and laughter. I'm told that a good belly laugh produces good chemicals that stay in the body for days. He has brought me many good laughs, too. I close with three of those.

I was asked to lead a four-day Gideon retreat near the Black Hills outside of Rapid City, South Dakota, in one of the most beautiful places in the country. Deer roamed the hills around the log cabins, and there was a huge meeting lodge that also served as a dining room. The cabins had no clocks or phones, and we were encouraged to just enjoy the time together, not worrying about the outside world. It was difficult at first, but we soon found ourselves at peace with it. We were given an agenda for meetings and meals, and a bell sounded when it was time to gather. Berdell had a conference to attend and wasn't with me.

Early on the third day after a run, I noticed a phone with no dial hanging on the outside lodge wall. Curious, I went over, picked up the phone and heard a recorded voice say, "At the sound of the tone, state your name." I was amazed.

At the tone, I obeyed: "John Ward."

"What number?" she said. I gave her my home phone number and heard the sound of a phone ringing. Berdell answered. The voice said, "This is a correctional facility. Will you accept charges on a call from," and then my recorded voice said "John Ward."

Berdell said "Oh, my goodness yes, I'll accept it! John, what in the world happened to you?"

I tried desperately to convince my wife that I wasn't in jail or prison, but she didn't seem convinced until I got home and explained the situation. When I hung up and told the Gideons at the camp what had happened, they laughed uncontrollably, explaining that the buildings had indeed been a correctional facility until a year before. Now the state rents it out for public functions. God has a sense of humor. I needed that laugh.

I was at another Gideon retreat in California, again in a rural setting with log cabins, a lodge meeting and dining room, and a gift shop. It was owned by a local church for use by Christian groups. A fellow Gideon and I were in the gift shop, and we noticed lots of hats on the wall for sale. One had the initials WWJD across the front. We hadn't seen that before, and the 80-year-old Gideon with me asked the man behind the counter, "What does WWJD stand for?"

"Oh, that stands for What Would Jesus Do."

The old man thought for a minute and said, "Well I know one thing he wouldn't do. He wouldn't pay $19.95 for that hat." Maybe I shouldn't have, but I laughed till my sides hurt.

Finally, as I returned from South America, landing at the Miami airport, I was standing at the luggage carrousel, waiting on my small bag when a TSA agent came by with a beagle sniff-dog looking for drugs. The little guy slowed down as he came near me, sniffing as if I were suspicious. The agent paused as she approached me, obviously responding to the dog. Suddenly I remembered those cocoa leaves that were still in my jacket pocket. I could see the headlines in all the papers, "International Chaplain of the Gideons BUSTED." Relieved when the agent moved on, I quickly went to the men's room and flushed the drugs down the toilet. That's what we druggies do when the narcs surprise us.

Epilogue

Berdell died at 61. Jeff, Wendy, and Kerry are believers and happily married to great people, and I have grands and great-grands. My wife, also Kerry, is a gift from God. I have so much for which to thank God, and tell Him so each morning. I start each day by standing outside and singing the "Doxology." Another lesson from Judge Digby.

In the Prologue, I wrote these words:

> It was Jesus who dared me to try things much bigger than I could have dreamed on my own. It was He who taught me that people who live within their own capabilities miss the reason why the Holy Spirit was given to us. We could have done ordinary things on our own.

If you have not experienced this partnership power, it is my prayer you will look for an opportunity to see it work. It seems to me to represent the real joy of knowing Christ that He wanted for us.

Have a great walk with God, and read Jeremiah 9:23-24 every Monday morning.

About the Author

John Ward was a successful trial lawyer for 24 years and a three-term Arkansas legislator, receiving the Bar Association's "Lawyer/Citizen" award. He was a trial judge for 14 years and received the Bar Association's "Outstanding Circuit Judge" honor.

He joined the Gideons International in 1987, serving both as State President and International Chaplain, and represented 14 Asian and 13 South American countries while having one of the busiest courts in the state. He was the featured speaker for the Houston, Texas, Mayor's Prayer Breakfast, where several lawyers and 13 judges made a profession of faith in Christ. He remains active as a Sunday school teacher and Gideon speaker. He lives with his wife, Kerry, in North Little Rock, Arkansas.

CPSIA information can be obtained
at www.ICGtesting.com
Printed in the USA
BVHW012128050623
665455BV00019B/529